CRUNCH MODE

YOURDON PRESS COMPUTING SERIES
Ed Yourdon, *Advisor*

BENTON AND WEEKES   *Program It Right: A Structured Method in BASIC*

BLOCK   *The Politics of Projects*

BODDIE   *Crunch Mode: Building Effective Systems on a Tight Schedule*

BRILL   *Building Controls Into Structured Systems*

BRILL   *Techniques of EDP Project Management: A Book of Readings*

CONSTANTINE AND YOURDON   *Structured Design: Fundamentals of a Discipline of Computer Program and Systems Design*

DE MARCO   *Concise Notes on Software Engineering*

DE MARCO   *Controlling Software Projects: Management, Measurement, and Estimates*

DE MARCO   *Structured Analysis and System Specification*

DICKINSON   *Developing Structured Systems: A Methodology Using Structured Techniques*

FLAVIN   *Fundamental Concepts in Information Modeling*

HANSEN   *Up and Running: A Case Study of Successful Systems Development*

KELLER   *Expert System Technology: Development and Application*

KELLER   *The Practice of Structured Analysis: Exploding Myths*

KING   *Current Practices in Software Development: A Guide to Successful Systems*

KRIEGER, POPPER, RIPPS, AND RADCLIFFE   *Structured Micro-Processor Programming*

MACDONALD   *Intuition to Implementation: Communicating About Systems Toward a Language of Structure in Data Processing System Development*

MC MENAMIN AND PALMER   *Essential Systems Analysis*

ORR   *Structured Systems Development*

PAGE-JONES   *The Practical Guide to Structured Systems Design*

PETERS   *Software Design: Methods and Techniques*

ROESKE   *The Data Factory: Data Center Operations and Systems Development*

SEMPREVIO   *Teams in Information Systems Development*

THOMSETT   *People and Project Management*

WARD   *Systems Development Without Pain: A User's Guide to Modeling Organizational Patterns*

WARD AND MELLOR   *Structured Development for Real-Time Systems, Volumes I, II, and III*

WEAVER   *Using the Structured Techniques: A Case Study*

WEINBERG   *Structured Analysis*

WELLS   *A Structured Approach to Building Programs: BASIC*

WELLS   *A Structured Approach to Building Programs: COBOL*

WELLS   *A Structured Approach to Building Programs: Pascal*

YOURDON   *Classics in Software Engineering*

YOURDON   *Coming of Age in the Land of Computers*

YOURDON   *Design of On-Line Computer Systems*

YOURDON, LISTER, GANE, AND SARSON   *Learning to Program in Structured Cobol, Parts 1 and 2*

YOURDON   *Managing Structured Techniques, 3/E*

YOURDON   *Managing the System Life Cycle*

YOURDON   *Structured Walkthroughs, 2/E*

YOURDON   *Techniques of Program Structure and Design*

YOURDON   *Writing of the Revolution: Selected Readings on Software Engineering*

ZAHN   *C Notes: A Guide to the C Programming*

CRUNCH MODE

Building Effective Systems
on a Tight Schedule

JOHN BODDIE

YOURDON PRESS
A Prentice-Hall Company
Englewood Cliffs, New Jersey 07632

Library of Congress Cataloging-in-Publication Data

BODDIE, JOHN.
    Crunch mode.

    (Yourdon Press computing series)
    Bibliography: p.
    Includes index.
    1. Computer software—Development. 2. System
design. I. Title. II. Series.
QA76.76.D47B63   1987   004.2   86-25593
ISBN 0-13-194960-8

Editorial/production supervision: *Denise Gannon*
Cover design: *Lundgren Graphics, Ltd.*
Manufacturing buyer: *Ed O'Dougherty*

Printed in the United States of America

10 9 8 7 6 5 4 3

ISBN 0-13-194960-8 025

PRENTICE-HALL INTERNATIONAL (UK) LIMITED, *London*
PRENTICE-HALL OF AUSTRALIA PTY. LIMITED, *Sydney*
PRENTICE-HALL CANADA INC., *Toronto*
PRENTICE-HALL HISPANOAMERICANA, S.A., *Mexico*
PRENTICE-HALL OF INDIA PRIVATE LIMITED, *New Delhi*
PRENTICE-HALL OF JAPAN, INC., *Tokyo*
PRENTICE-HALL OF SOUTHEAST ASIA PTE. LTD., *Singapore*
EDITORA PRENTICE-HALL DO BRASIL, LTDA., *Rio de Janeiro*

This book is dedicated,
with love and respect,
to my parents.

CONTENTS

PREFACE   x

ACKNOWLEDGMENTS   xiii

A BRIEF NOTE ON NAMES   xvi

Chapter 1   THEORY AND PRACTICE   1

System Development as a Business
    Decision 4
Reality and its Consequences 6
Hope for the Present 8

Chapter 2   GOING IN   9

The Search for Essentials 13
The Role of the Customer 17
Specification as an Ongoing Activity 19
The Limits of the Possible 20

Chapter 3   THE FIRST CUT   **23**

The Role of the Initial Presentation 25
Presentation Tools 30
The Geography of the System 33
Response and Rework 36
The Project Team and the
    Presentation 37
The Importance of "Top-Down"
    Thinking 38

Chapter 4   SCHEDULES AND ESTIMATES   **41**

The Fruits of Software Estimating 43
A Different Kind of Estimating 45
The Development Road Map 47
Interlude 53
Sink or Swim 55
Avoiding Compromise 57
Milestones and Tombstones 58
Some Estimating Heuristics 58
Dive and Surface 60
Ignoring the Budget 62
A Look Backward at the Scheduling
    Process 63

Chapter 5   PROGRAMMING UNDER PRESSURE   **65**

Foundation Stones 68
A Brief Discourse on Method 71
Data Dictionaries 74
Specification and Design Languages 77
Recent Developments 81
Brave Old World 84
The Choice of a Programming
    Language 87
Top-Down and Outside-In 92
Life Without Walkthroughs 97
Where is the Magic? 99

Chapter 6   THE LIGHT BRIGADE   101

The Pressures on Individuals 103
Project Leaders 107
Project Managers 109
Assembling the Team 111
Selling the Project 112
The Shape of the Team 114
Hired Guns 115
Benefits Now 117
Generalities 120

Chapter 7   FLOATING IN THE RAPIDS   121

Overtime 123
The Testing Process and Project
     Control 126
Controlling Unit Testing 128
System Testing as the Project Control
     Function 131
Putting the Pieces Together 134
Small Victories and Celebrations 135
Running Interference 137
System Debugging 139
A Parting Shot 141

Chapter 8   DEALING WITH DISASTER   143

Missed Milestones and Their
     Consequences 146
Don't Kid Yourself 149
"Floating" Specifications 149
People Problems 151
Burnout 154
Strategic Withdrawal 155

Chapter 9   ARRIVING ON TIME   159

Documentation 161
Training 163

Installation 165
Preparing for Maintenance 165
The Feedback File 166
The Project Post-Mortem 167
Reviewing the Troops 168

Appendix   **BRIEF DESCRIPTIONS OF DESIGN
            TOOLS**   **169**

Data Flow Diagrams 171
Structure Charts 173
Nassi-Shneiderman Diagrams 174
Action Diagrams 175
Structured English and Pseudocode 177
Warnier-Orr Diagrams 178

NOTES   **181**

INDEX   **187**

PREFACE

The ability to get working software quickly into the hands of users will be characteristic of successful data processing organizations for the foreseeable future. Groups that can produce and install software systems within tight time frames will prosper. Those which can't will fail and, in some cases, they will bring the enterprises of which they are a part down with them. Fast response to changing information processing requirements is a necessity in today's world.

Rapid software development is possible and manageable. As we will see, it's getting easier than it used to be. Software produced within very tight time frames need not be "quick and dirty." Quality and short development times are not mutually exclusive.

This book is not a pitch for some great new software package to help you produce software in one-tenth of the time it used to take. While many tools are available to make the development process faster and easier, some of the most valuable tools for rapid development have been around for over a decade. We'll spend some time with these established techniques and take a look at some new ones.

Developing software in "crunch mode"—with a schedule that puts you under pressure from the first day of the project—is unlike other kinds of software development. It changes the people who participate in it and it changes the people who manage it. Some people seem to thrive when working in crunch mode; others are unable to perform. Managing the project team can be challenging, exciting, frustrating, rewarding, and tiring. A considerable part of the book is devoted to the problems of management in a "crunch mode" environment.

This book is intended for anyone who must manage a crunch-mode project or who happens to be caught up in the middle of one. We will follow a real project—the development of the first on-track account betting system installed in the United States. The system was designed, staffed, programmed, tested, and installed in 100 calendar days and proved to be effectively error free.

This result was not achieved by "superprogrammers." The development was not without false starts, errors, and other problems. It was not achieved in an environment with powerful software development tools or unlimited hardware resources. If you are going into your first crunch-mode project, you will encounter many of the situations described in this book. If you've been through a crunch-mode project before, the book may bring back fond memories, and it will help you avoid some unpleasant ones in the future.

The focus of this book is productivity. Not productivity as measured in "lines of code per week" or some other sterile statistic, but as the ability to get working software "out the door" in a hurry. You will find some interesting approaches to increasing productivity and some examples of methods to avoid. As you read, think about your current project. There's probably something in the book you can apply to the work you're doing now. Try it out. A little gain in productivity can do wonders for your project, your attitude, and your career.

JOHN BODDIE

ACKNOWLEDGMENTS

Thank you

To the project teams I've been part of over the years—these groups were the forge where the basic concepts in this book were hammered out. They are also where some lifelong friends were found. Looking back, I feel somewhat dazed at my good fortune in being associated with as varied and talented a bunch of people as exists in this business.

To the managers who taught me more than they, or I, realized at the time—specifically, to George Matkovits at Control Data Corporation, Tony Brookfield at Mohawk Data Sciences, Harvey Dubner at Dubner Computer Systems and Jack DeVries at General Instrument.

To Phil Mellor for allowing me to make use of his excellent library.

To Linda Shelhamer of United Totalizator, who kindly gave me permission to use the Call-a-Bet system as the project example.

To Mary Kwasnik, a first-class designer and first-class friend who provided some excellent suggestions early in the writing process.

To Dr. Donald Deutsch, who introduced me to computing.

To Ed Yourdon, who took the effort to respond to an unsolicited letter.

To the people at Yourdon, Inc., particularly Dan Mausner, who provided the editorial guidance I sorely needed.

To Denise Gannon of Prentice-Hall, who went through crunch mode to turn my manuscript into this book.

And finally, but by no means least, to my wife and children for more things than I could put in a book three times this size.

A Brief Note on Names

The names used in describing the development of the Dynatote Call-a-Bet system are not the names of the individuals who actually worked on the project.

Throughout the book, the pronouns "she" and "he," "his" and "hers," and "him" and "her" should be thought of as interchangeable. Any reasonable project leader knows productivity is not predetermined by gender.

Chapter 1

THEORY
AND
PRACTICE

More software projects have gone awry for lack of
calendar time than for all other causes combined.

F.P. Brooks, Jr.
The Mythical Man-Month[1]

"Harris, we both know the order tracking system needs to be overhauled. Well, the word has come down that it needs to be done now, before the Christmas orders start coming in. That gives us about ninety days to get the new system in place. It's a tight schedule, but I'm sure you can come up with a way to do it. I shouldn't need to tell you that this is the most visible project in the company. You'll have whatever you need to get the job done. I want to get together with you at the end of next week to review your schedules in detail."

Chances are, Harris feels a block of ice where his stomach used to be.

Many of us know what Harris is going through. We can foresee what life is going to be like for him and his team over the next ninety days. They're going to be in "crunch mode," trying to get six months of work delivered in three. Stories of crunch mode are common in the computer business. It's unlikely anyone in the business for more than five years has entirely avoided crunch mode. Most of us feel it's only a matter of time before we see it again.

In an ideal world there would be no crunch mode. Projects would be planned, designed, and implemented in an orderly fashion. Managers would set up schedules allowing the job to be done right the first time. Management would see the advantages in this approach and would save countless dollars otherwise spent for maintenance and revision. Stories of

100-hour weeks and inflexible deadlines would become computing folk-lore, like knowing how to read punched cards by looking at the holes.

There is no shortage of literature dealing with management of com-puter projects. The quality of the material is generally high. Many ideas and approaches are presented. Most have been tried and have been success-ful under proper conditions. Unfortunately for our friend Harris, many of the proper conditions will be absent.

This book is written to help anyone who, like Harris, finds himself or herself facing crunch mode. It is not a formula approach. It's a collection of observations and practices gathered from successful crunch-mode proj-ects—not all of them will apply to your situation. In order to see some of the practices in action, we are going to follow a real project, a transaction processing system used at racetracks. The system was designed, pro-grammed, tested, and installed in 100 days.

System Development as a Business Decision

Before we look at techniques for managing crunch mode, we should take a little time to understand how it comes about. Contrary to opinions held by many programmers, crunch-mode projects are neither the result of gross incompetence nor abysmal insensitivity on the part of management. They are the natural consequence of the way business decisions are made.

The decision to build a new system is a business decision. The benefits from having the system are expected to outweigh the cost and inconven-ience of building it. As with most business decisions, costs and benefits are not clearly known when the project begins. Considerable risk is involved. The architects of a project completed on time and within budget may find that the expected benefits never materialize. There are plenty of "software Edsels."

A characteristic of business decisions that affects almost all systems projects is a concern for timing. Let's suppose a study of the business shows a new order tracking system is needed to handle the Christmas rush, which peaks in October. The system must be ready by the time the rush starts. If it isn't finished until early December, after the rush is over, the benefits ex-pected will not be realized. The project will be considered a failure, even though the software itself may be first-rate, because the primary objective was not accomplished—the new system did not help the company handle the Christmas rush.

Costs and benefits are easier to see for short-term projects than they are for long-term. Implicit in short-term benefit analysis is the assumption that the new product or system will be available quickly. The benefits of being the first to bring a new product or service to market can be substantial.

American Totalizator Systems provides computers and software used at racetracks. In 1977 the company developed a new type of system, one where the person who took your bet could also pay out your winnings. Previously these functions were performed by different people. The development schedule was extremely tight. Shortly after the system was completed, the major racetracks in the New York City area and the Meadowlands, the largest track in New Jersey, selected new systems. American Totalizator's rapid development had left it in the position of being the only company capable of supplying this new type of system. The system was selected for each of these racetracks. On a good day, these tracks handle a total of over $4 million in bets. Companies supplying racetrack systems are paid a percentage of the total money wagered—rapid product development was a key factor in realizing these benefits of American Totalizator's business decision.

The ability to recognize opportunity and respond quickly to it is common to many successful enterprises. Sometimes the opportunity is found, other times it is created. Tom Peters and Nancy Austin devote a section of their book, *A Passion for Excellence*, to the subject of innovation.[2] They conclude the key to innovation is to be found in small, self-contained "skunk works" teams. What's special about these teams? The authors point out that they seem to do things in an exceptionally short period of time. The ability of a company to take quick advantage of new technologies, new markets and new ideas is a recurring theme in studies of business success. Given this, it's surprising that crunch mode doesn't arrive more often.

In today's world, more and more companies are concerned with "time to market" as a factor in their planning. Companies in the telecommunications, instrumentation, and computer industries are particularly sensitive to this issue. The product life in these industries is getting shorter, which makes it increasingly important to develop new products in time for announcement at trade shows and conventions where they will receive maximum publicity. The software incorporated in the new products must be produced in time to allow the planned marketing effort to be effective. In many cases, a company will have several crunch-mode projects active at one time.

In some cases crunch mode is not a matter of opportunity—it's a matter of survival. American Totalizator's chief competitor in the racetrack system business is Autotote, Inc. When American Totalizator's new system was announced, Autotote didn't have a comparable product. Autotote's management knew they would need one, and fast. They were losing their customer base. Talk about pressure. One of the Autotote team members recalls,

It was about 2:30 Saturday morning when the engineering director came up behind me and asked, "How's it going?" I'd been working on a particularly nasty bug and it was really getting me down. So I told him I didn't think we had a chance of meeting the target date. I found out the next day my comment had started a crisis meeting which included the president and all the vice-presidents. They were scared to death I might be right.

The atmosphere in which business decisions take place seems to be getting even more volatile. New products and services are introduced at a tremendous rate. Just think about the developments in a "conservative" industry like banking and the number of new systems banks have required. This state of affairs is likely to continue.[3] Organizations and managers who can deal with crunch mode effectively should have many successful years in front of them.

Reality and its Consequences

Harris, who got his orders at the beginning of this chapter, is going to find out that his project will differ in many ways from those described in his software management books. This realization won't be long in coming.

Most books on project management start by stressing the importance of clearly defined system requirements. After all, you can't build a system if you don't know what it's supposed to do. Or can you? The stated requirement for Harris is to build a new order tracking system in ninety days or less. This requirement acts as an umbrella for many detailed requirements in the areas of reporting, inquiry, file maintenance, and inventory management. On a short-term project, not all the requirements may be known. The system may be delivered with some secondary requirements unfulfilled. New requirements will be discovered as the project moves forward. Harris will need to get comfortable with the idea of building a useful but incomplete system.

Since the requirements are subject to change, the system specifications can never be "frozen." Harris and his group will be shooting at a moving target. This problem will not affect only the programmers—the people responsible for documentation, user training, and system testing will also need to revise their plans to keep up with changes in the specification.

Requirements and specification tasks comprise what we know as "systems analysis." We are all aware of the dangers of development based on incomplete or imperfect analysis. But analysis takes time and the analysis task, like all other tasks in a crunch-mode project, will have only limited time to yield a result. With only ninety days available, Harris may be forced to rely on whatever analysis has been completed by the twenty-day point. The design will wind up being influenced by a factor with no logical relationship to the functions the system must perform.

Once the system analysis, such as it is, has been "completed," the job of system design begins. Harris would like to turn the work over to his chief programmer, but he doesn't have a chief programmer. In fact, there isn't a chief programmer in the company. Despite promises he can have whatever he needs to get the job done, Harris can't get Alice transferred from the credit-check project. It's not that the project team is a collection of misfits; it has some pretty good people. Harris has worked with some of them before. But he can see right now he won't be able to set up a "chief programmer team." Another structure is required, and the success of the project will depend on Harris's ability to find one.

As design moves forward, programming can start. Here at least there are not too many problems. Most of the staff has been exposed to structured programming methods and can be relied upon to use them. Unfortunately, members of the staff are not in complete agreement as to what constitutes structured programs. Software review sessions start chewing up inordinate amounts of time and occasionally degenerate into arguments about details of coding style. A review of the code shows wide differences in standard operations like I/O, error handling, and in both the quality and quantity of comments.

The staff assigned to test the system now gets to look at the first functions to come out of the programming group. They are not pleased. Some of the functions they expected are missing, and other functions operate differently than they'd envisioned. The user documentation group gets wind of the differences and begins to wonder aloud if the project is in control. Criticism of this sort does not endear the test and documentation groups to the programmers. While testing and programming are meant to function as adversaries, open hostility threatens to cripple the project.

As individual programmers turn over their work to be integrated into the system, Harris encounters some unexpected problems. Angela's order-archive program was unit-tested using a customer file that didn't include credit history information. It seems she worked the weekend and wasn't around Monday morning when the file change was agreed upon. Somehow she didn't get the word. The amount of time required to generate and control test data is turning out to be much longer than Harris expected.

The ninety-day clock continues to tick. Early in the project, if an item was a day or two late, Harris could convince himself the time could be made up somehow. He can't do that now. He talks to the team about a last, big push, but the team is pushing as hard as it can. He doesn't know what else he can do.

Hope for the Present

Project managers like Harris find themselves "between a rock and a hard place." On one side is a set of methodologies that assume sufficient time for proper system development. A project manager for one of America's fifty largest companies commented on the detailed methodology used in his division: "With all the design documents and walkthroughs and reviews and follow-ups we have to do, we couldn't get a ten-line COBOL program out the door in less than three weeks."

On the other side, turning away from advances in development techniques raises the risk of a return to the "good old days" where programmers worked at cross-purposes and "tricky" code was a sign of expertise. Gains in productivity and program reliability have come hard to the computer industry, and few managers want to give them up.

Things look bleak. There does not appear to be a middle ground between current methodology and the time pressure forced upon many programming projects. Nevertheless, some systems are built quickly and they work when delivered. Some managers and programming teams seem to work well in pressure situations.

These groups have not developed a new set of methods for system development. What they have done is to carefully select elements of current technical practice, modifying tools and techniques to meet specific project requirements. These groups have also recognized the relationship between productivity and management style. In this area, too, they have adopted practices that work for the project at hand. There is no set formula that, when followed, will guarantee even the best of groups can produce miracles on demand—there are only tools and techniques that can give you a better chance of surviving crunch mode with your system, your team, and even your sense of humor intact.

Chapter 2

GOING IN

In the weeks that followed this encounter with Enderby, George Smiley found himself in a complex and variable mood to accompany his many tasks of preparation. He was not at peace; he was not, in a single phrase, definable as a single person, beyond the one constant thrust of his determination. . . . Among those who remembered him later—most, in their various ways, spoke of an ominous *going in*, a *quietness*, an economy of word or glance, and they described it according to their knowledge of him, and their station in life.

John Le Carre
Smiley's People[1]

The first steps taken in a crunch-mode project will establish a tone and direction for the project and will have a considerable influence on the ultimate chances of success. This is a difficult time for the project leader. She will be taking most of the actions alone. The myriad problems and time pressures facing her can lead to an overwhelming desire to "start something now."

This desire must be held in check. If you find yourself leading a crunch-mode project, the first thing you must do is take time and think. Leave your office, take a walk, do whatever works for you to set up conditions where you can think about the project as an entity. Don't let yourself get bogged down in details. What do you know about the project? What do you need to find out?

The beginning of the project is the time to do some "general systems thinking." The term was coined by Gerald Weinberg, who has written several excellent books on the subject.[2] General systems thinking forces you to think not only about the software system you must build, but also about the human, social, and business worlds of which the system will be a part. The goal of this type of thinking is a better understanding of the system, as opposed to a better knowledge of it.

This differentiation between "knowledge of a system" and "understanding of a system" is not a trivial semantic issue. By seeking to understand the system, you need to think about how it will be used and how it will affect both the people who use it and the nature of the work they do. This understanding gives you a context for making the many design and implementation decisions required in the development process (see Figure 2-1).

It might be helpful to think of the understanding of a system as an "outside view"—it looks at the system as an entity. Knowledge of the system concerns itself with details within the system—it's the "inside view." Once the development gets under way, most of your thinking will use the inside view of the system. If you haven't taken the time to develop an outside view, you will have a great deal of difficulty evaluating the many suggestions to change the system that arise during the development period.

It's time to introduce the system we'll be following for the rest of the book.

November 11, 1980

The Dynatote on-track account betting project was started in November of 1980. Dynatote had contracted earlier to provide a system, dubbed "Call-a-Bet," to Louisville Downs. The system would let the track's customers maintain accounts at the track and place bets over the phone.

The contract required building a system that would allow a customer to open an account at the track in person or by mail. An initial deposit would be required, and the account holder could make additional deposits by mail or in person. If checks were submitted as deposits, Louisville Downs would hold them for several days to allow them to clear before crediting the deposit to the account balance. To place a bet, the account holder would call an operator at the track and give his account number and his individual password. He could then place bets for the races to be run that evening. As each bet was made, the cost of the bet would be deducted from his account balance. After each race, the system would adjust the balances in accounts with winning bets placed on the race, adding the amount won to the current balance. A customer could request a withdrawal from his account in person or through the mail. All withdrawals would be paid by check.

By November it was clear that the programming staff originally proposed would not be able to complete the new system on time. Ben, a project manager with experience in racetrack systems, was assigned to lead the Call-a-Bet project. A junior programmer was assigned to help him. A design presentation was scheduled for representatives of Louisville Downs in ten days.

Ben asked to see both the contractual documents and the design work done to date. The contract was very general. There was no coherent existing design.

Figure 2-1. "Understanding" and "Knowing" a System.

Consider Ben's first step. First, he asked to see the contract, the item that made the system a required product. The contract stated the delivery dates and the mandatory requirements that bounded the development effort. Most important, the contract gave Ben an idea of what the customer was expecting from the delivered product.

The Search for Essentials

What was Ben trying to accomplish? He was beginning a process that would give him a clear idea of the essential features of the system, the ones needed to deliver a product that satisfied the true needs of the customer.[3] The general language of the contract was both a blessing and a curse in this regard.

It was a blessing in that it gave Ben a great deal of control over what would be delivered. Since he would write the specification, decisions as to the features included or left out would go through him. The customer was placed in a position of reacting to his proposals, giving Ben a strong position in the negotiations common to most crunch-mode projects.

It was a curse in that Ben had no guidelines as to what the customer expected. He would be putting in ten days effort to develop a specification that might be rejected out of hand. Ben wasn't too worried about this because he knew a lot about the industry, but this was the first system of its type, and he had no way of knowing if the customer believed certain features had been promised.

A contract that includes a system specification, either as an integral part of the contract or as a request for proposal referenced by the contract, can be a two-edged sword for the project leader. If it is well done, it can give information about the project requirements that allows the project leader to go directly to the software design activities. Unfortunately, good specifications are rare. If you are given a large and detailed specification at the beginning of a crunch-mode project, be alert to some pitfalls:

• The contract may contain a lot of extraneous detail about the current system. You will need to wade through this detail to find out what the essential features of the system are. You may get caught in the trap of believing that every detail mentioned in the contract is mandatory for the new system. This is seldom true. Systems that have existed for several years will almost always contain functions that are no longer used and features that operate in such a way as to "get around" restrictions in the original system.

• The contract may leave out important information. Recently I reviewed a request for proposal from a transportation company that provided cash advances to long-distance truckers. The RFP, which would have become part of the contract, gave a detailed description of the current system. After going through it for the first time, I had the uncomfortable feeling I had missed something. I was halfway through reading it the second time when I suddenly realized it did not mention internal financial controls. I brought this up when I met with the customer and was told I should propose "appropriate" controls in the delivered system.

• The contract may give detailed descriptions of certain features of the system and, at the same time, be very vague about others. This can leave a misleading impression of customer expectations. Differences in emphasis are particular problems in technical descriptions written by groups of people. The perceived emphasis may reflect nothing more than differences in writing ability among the team members who wrote the specifications.

It is the responsibility of the project leader to define the essentials of the product to be delivered. This is best approached as an individual task.

The project leader must demonstrate leadership right at the beginning. She must be able to explain to the project team what the system is to do and why it must be done. By doing this at the very beginning, she provides a focus for the project team.

November 12, 1980

The Call-a-Bet system was going to function as a "front-end" to an existing totalizator. A totalizator is a computer at a racetrack that records all the bets, calculates the odds, and figures out the final prices once the race has been run and the winners are known.

Since the Call-a-Bet system would be a front-end, Ben realized he wouldn't need to worry about maintaining a complete set of parimutuel information, such as the amount bet on each horse. The system would be concerned primarily with accounts. He would need to balance financial activity in the Call-a-Bet system with activity reported in the totalizator, but this was much less effort than developing a duplicate totalizator.

With the limited amount of information he had, Ben drew a diagram, shown here as Figure 2-2. As diagrams go, it's not much to look at. That hardly means it's unimportant. The diagram establishes the boundaries between Call-a-Bet and the world outside it. It shows the system as something separate from the totalizator and shows that users can make deposits and withdrawals. This drawing is the starting point. It will remain a true representation of the system no matter how many details we add to the Call-a-Bet design.

As the design becomes more refined there will be many opportunities to add functions to it. The project leader must often act as a "devil's advocate" in evaluating suggested enhancements. "What would we do if we couldn't provide this report? What would the operator do if he didn't have this piece of information?" The project leader must be careful to see that the team asks the same questions about her brilliant suggestions as well.

Adding functions onto the system can get out of hand quickly if it isn't controlled. The project leader must constantly look for ways to minimize the scope of the work to be done. The president of a software firm makes the point this way:

> Building a system is a lot like carving the statue of an elephant. You get a big block of marble and cut away everything that doesn't look like an elephant. The problem with most systems is that people want to put a howdah on the elephant's back and a maharajah in it and before you know it eighty percent of the effort is going into designing the rings on the maharajah's left hand.

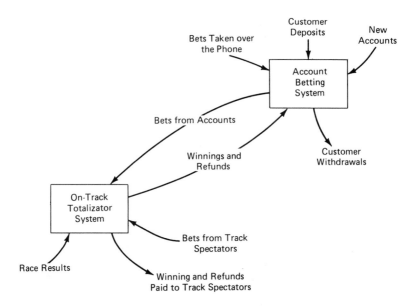

Figure 2–2.   The Call-a-Bet System Environment.

November 16, 1980

Ben picked up speed after the first couple of days. He had a clear idea of what the system needed to do to handle customer accounts and an idea of how the interface to the totalizator would work. He had given some thought to the controls the system would require.

He had collected a number of small drawings of pieces of the system. Some of them looked like data flow diagrams, others looked like Warnier-Orr diagrams*, and still others looked like a collage of several different methods. The meeting with the customer was six days off. It was time to pull things together.

Ben got a pile of large posterboards and a collection of markers in several different colors. He began to lay out a series of high-level data flow diagrams. These would be his tools in presenting the system to the customer. They also had another purpose—they would force Ben to take his thoughts about the new system and put them into a formal context. The design was not clearly worked out in Ben's head before the task of putting it on paper started. By putting them down as part of a presentation, Ben could see areas he had overlooked and other areas that were nice but not necessary.

---

*A brief overview of these techniques can be found in the appendix.

At this point, focus is the key. How is the system to be used? What is the product? What is the minimum system needed to do the job? Correct answers to these questions can only come from "understanding the system."

Remember, the time allowed to complete the project is limited. No matter how productive the project team is, there is a limit to what can be accomplished. Every additional function strains that limit. There will be a number of suggestions related to functions that aren't absolutely necessary but would make the system more attractive to the customer or the end user. Rather than shooting these suggestions down in flames, the project leader should leave open the opportunity to include them if the schedule clearly allows it. If the project is finished and operational on time but doesn't include the "nice" features, the customer may grumble. But if you commit to the features at the beginning of the project and then find you can't deliver on time, the grumble may be replaced with a roar.

Dynatote was fortunate to have Ben as the project leader. Since Ben had considerable experience with racetrack systems, he was able to put himself in the user's place as he thought about the features the system needed. In most cases, the project leader will need to spend considerable time with the customer before she understands the system's true requirements.

The Role of the Customer

The customer is the person or group exercising ultimate control over the project. His is the voice that can kill the project. If you're designing a system for a large organization, it may be difficult to figure out who the customer is. If you're presented with a project needing approval from multiple departments or groups, demand that the groups agree on a single spokesperson before you commit to anything. For a crunch-mode project, it is absolutely essential to have only one customer. There is no such thing as a rush job requiring six different approvals. The time needed to get all parties to agree may take longer than the time required to actually build the system.[4]

The project leader and the customer are likely to start off speaking different languages. They will be using terminology based on their view of the world in which the system will operate. Every industry or service has its own body of knowledge and custom—this is the "folklore" the project leader must understand before she can work effectively with the customer. If the project leader doesn't already know the folklore, one of the best things she can do is relate what she understands about the customer's project to another application she is more familiar with.

I was called in to help with development of a system to handle information in a clinical laboratory. A clinical laboratory performs tests on body tissues and fluids and reports the results of these tests to your doctor. I knew nothing of the clinical laboratory business. Nevertheless, after a couple of days I learned enough to tell the software manager I thought I understood what he was doing. "Good," he said, "I have people who have worked here for five years who don't understand it. Let's hear you explain it." I told him he was building cars.

I went on, "At a car factory in Detroit, an order comes in from a dealer in Atlanta. He wants a car with a set of options. But once the order gets into the factory, nobody's working on a car. Some of them are working on brake assemblies, others are working on rear axles, others are putting in windshields, but there's nobody whose job it is to 'build a car.' It's the same thing in your labs. Orders come in; some want to test blood sugar, others are looking for cancer cells, others are checking for poisons. Inside the lab you have groups working on hematology, groups working on cytology, and groups working on toxicology. None of those groups has the responsibility to 'run the tests for this order.' In the car factory, the end result is a car that rolls off the assembly line and is sent to Atlanta. In your lab, the end result is a report of the tests performed and their results, which is sent to the doctor."

The technique of relating a customer's system to a system you already know about is a useful one, and it's usually not difficult. The range of computer applications is not quite as large as we might like to believe. Handling automatic teller machines for a bank is not entirely unlike handling bets at a racetrack. A closed-loop control system to handle gasoline blending at a refinery is quite similar to a system controlling the thickness of paper in a paper mill. Think about the last system you worked on. Did it have similarities to other systems you know about?

If you can find a reference point in another industry or application, it can help you to avoid misunderstandings. When customers give direct explanations of what they require they may leave out basic information. They don't do this to make the project leader's life more difficult—they do it because they're thinking about it in terms of the world they work in. If asked to relate their activities to analogous activities in another system, they need to "step outside" the world they're familiar with. Points of difference and similarity can then be used by the project leader to figure out what's really needed.

In the next chapter, we'll look at the approach of making presentations of the system. Using graphic material in a presentation environment is a very effective way of working with the customer. He can react to graphic representations of the proposed system and point out specific areas where your understanding is faulty. From the standpoint of time, this is likely to be much more effective than simply asking questions. Furthermore, since the customer is reacting to something tangible, it's easier for him to feel as if he is an integral part of the development of the new system.

If you are part of an enterprise where crunch-mode projects occur frequently, you might take some time between projects to learn about some specification tools that have proved effective in reducing the time needed to identify the requirements for a new system. *JAD* (Joint Application Design) from IBM, *Consensus* from Boeing Computer Services, *The Method* from Performance Resources, and *Wisdm* from Wise, Inc. are examples of requirements methodology products. CNA Insurance Co. performed a test of one of these products and found that it reduced the time to develop requirements and external design by two-thirds.[5]

People who sell and use these products make it clear that training is required to use them effectively. The training is necessary not only for the data processing group, but also for the customers. The products guide the interaction between designers and customers during the requirements process, and both the system designer and the customer must be familiar with the methodology for the full benefit to be realized.

It may seem a minor point, but at this point you should try to think of a short name or acronym for the system. During development, the Dynatote Call-a-Bet system was called TABS (Telephone Account Betting System). A system for a bank was called CATS (Customer Account Transaction System). A "system nickname" helps to personalize the system and makes talking about it easier. See if the customer has a name in mind. Encourage members of the project team to come up with a name. Help make it *their* system.

Specification as an On-Going Activity

In a crunch-mode project, the requirements of the system are seldom fully defined by the time detailed design and coding are started. The project leader should make it a habit to continue to talk to the customer on a regular basis, rechecking assumptions and probing for additional detail. Additional information always seems to turn up in these conversations. Some of the new information will force you to change your assumptions about the way the system should work. This is all to the good. You certainly do not want to commit the amount of mental and physical effort required for a crunch-mode effort only to find you've produced a useless system.

Remember, specification changes do not always need to be additive. The project leader should always be on the lookout for functions to be postponed until a future level. She should be alert to possible redundancies in the current system design. For instance, two separate reports are defined for the controller's office—couldn't they be combined?

If the project leader has done her work well, she will come out of the first few weeks with a good understanding of what is required. She will have set an example for development practices to be followed by the group. She will now have a decent working relationship with the customer. The only item remaining is delivery of the system on the date promised.

The Limits of the Possible

The combination of excellent technical staff, superb management, outstanding designers, and intelligent, committed customers is not enough to guarantee success for a crunch-mode project. There really are such things as impossible projects. New ones are started every day. Most impossible projects can be recognized as such very early in the development cycle. There seem to be two major types: "poorly understood systems" and "very complex systems."

A "poorly understood system" is a system that's poorly understood by the system designer and/or the customer. There may be several reasons for this:

• The designer may have difficulty comprehending the true customer requirements. This can be a result of problems in communication between the designer and the customer. If the customer is using terms the designer is not familiar with and no common ground can be found, a gap is almost certain to exist between the customer's expectations and the designer's plans.

• The customer may insist on an approach the designer doesn't agree with. Alternatively, the designer may favor an approach that leaves the customer uncomfortable. Again, this may be due to difficulties in communicating the nature of the problems to be solved. It may also be based on a desire to use an approach that worked in a different situation.

• The customer may have unrealistic expectations for the system. This sometimes happens when computers are being introduced to a new area in the enterprise. A friend of mine was recently asked to contribute to the design of an "office automation system." To do what the customer actually wanted, a full-scale order and inventory tracking system was required.

• The customer may want to solve a number of different problems through the development of a single system.

It is a mistake for the project to proceed as a crunch-mode effort if the designer feels she doesn't understand the requirements clearly. This is not to say the system shouldn't be built at all, but it shouldn't be pushed forward with all possible speed. If it is, the result may be a system that must be discarded because it doesn't do what the customer needs it to.

We must recognize the difference between not knowing all the requirements of the system and not understanding the requirements as we see them. The first is quite normal in crunch-mode development. The requirements that are not known will seldom conflict with the ones that are known, and in many cases the requirements uncovered later in development can be "set aside" to be dealt with in a subsequent upgrade to the system as initially delivered.

Not understanding the requirements as they are perceived is a much more serious problem. If design proceeds from this point, the system may be fatally flawed. If the designer feels she doesn't have a good understanding of the system, she must be forthright and say so. It may be difficult to ask for more time to define the system when the customer is pressing to get started, but it must be done.

A second class of systems that may be inappropriate for crunch-mode development is "very complex systems." With these systems, the requirements may be understood clearly, the preferred design approach may be obvious, and the techniques for implementing the design may be well known. The problem is that there is too much to be done in a limited time.

Fortunately, very complex systems are fairly rare. Edsger Dijkstra makes this point when he writes,

> Although large, advanced, and sophisticated programming efforts are more spectacular, we must not forget that quite a lot of machine time and programmer's energy is really spent on small, down-to-earth projects and the present efforts to make computing facilities more directly accessible to the individual user will only reinforce this tendency.[6]

Systems with performance constraints often fall into the class of very complex systems because of the amount of detailed work necessary to achieve optimum performance. In some cases, the software will require changes to the computer's operating system to reach the required performance levels. Very large systems are poor candidates for crunch-mode development because of the amount of time required for the various groups working on the system to coordinate their activities. Individual parts of the very large system can be done in crunch mode, but only after the interfaces between these parts and the rest of the system are thoroughly defined.

Systems based on new technology can benefit from a crunch-mode approach to develop prototypes for a system, but these crunch-mode prototypes often have shortcomings that should be corrected before the system is released for production use. Most prototype systems of this sort show evidence of "false starts" based on misunderstandings about the new technology. In virtually every case, the people who built the prototype will see simpler and "cleaner" ways to build the final system.

Chapter 3

THE FIRST
CUT

It's what you learn after you know it all that
counts.

John Wooden

Successful systems are not developed in a vacuum. With crunch-mode systems, as with other systems, there comes a point where the designer must present the products of his effort for general appraisal. It is through this presentation and review process that the system gets truly defined and the people who are to build it and use it come to understand both the purpose and the nature of their undertaking.

With crunch-mode projects, the initial presentation should take place quickly. The attention of the customer is strongly focused upon the project, and the designer's concepts should not be so rigid that change is resisted. It is important for the designer to take the lead in this process. By presenting the system for review, he helps establish his control of the development process. Further, the need to organize the presentation forces him to bring together his thoughts about the system and turn them into a design.

The Role of the Initial Presentation

The first cut at the system design must identify the inputs to the system, the outputs from the system, and the primary files or data stores main-

---

November 17, 1980

Ben went through a lot of poster board and marks on the whiteboard during the days preceding the meeting with the representatives from Louisville Downs. In the end, he had a set of diagrams describing the functions of the system and the interconnections between the various parts. He made some reduced copies of the drawings for handouts at the presentation, but he didn't prepare any written material.

He didn't have any time to prepare written material. Writing takes a lot of time compared to drawing and offers far more opportunities for misunderstanding. In addition, he needed materials for a presentation. It is difficult to have an effective presentation if you must use phrases like, "If you'll look at paragraph two on page five, you'll see what we intend to do about overdrafts." What he needed was a medium where the customer could get directly involved without a lot of preparation. Furthermore, Ben knew he might need to make changes in the design as a result of the presentation. With a set of data flow diagrams, he could lay out some of the changes right in front of the customer. He could get reaction without delay.

The actual presentation for the customer went very smoothly. Louisville Downs sent the two officials who would be most concerned with the new system to the conference. One was to be in charge of the Call-a-Bet operation and the other was responsible for all the money bet and paid out during the races. Both had extensive backgrounds in racetrack management.

The presentation provided clarification in the areas of handling deposits by check and treatment of checks which bounced. It also brought out the fact the State of Kentucky required a printed record of each bet made at the time it was made. Changes in the design to accomodate the new requirements were sketched in.

---

tained in the system. Detailed descriptions are not required; in fact, they may get in the way. It is enough to identify something called the account file and indicate it contains account holder information, current balance, and account status. Figures 3-1, 3-2, and 3-3 show the level of detail provided in the first presentation for the Call-a-Bet system.

The first cut must do an adequate job of presenting the system so its parts can be recognized. Just as important, the first cut must make it possible to identify pieces that are missing. A graphic presentation is by far the best way to do this. At this level, systems are visualized as organic wholes made from identifiable parts. When you see the word "crocodile," what do you think of? Do you think of "any of a family of large, flesh-eating lizard-like reptiles living in the water and on the muddy banks of tropical

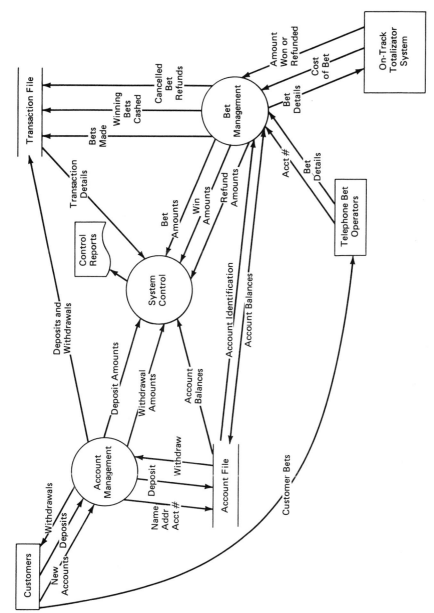

Figure 3-1. Account Betting System Overview.

27

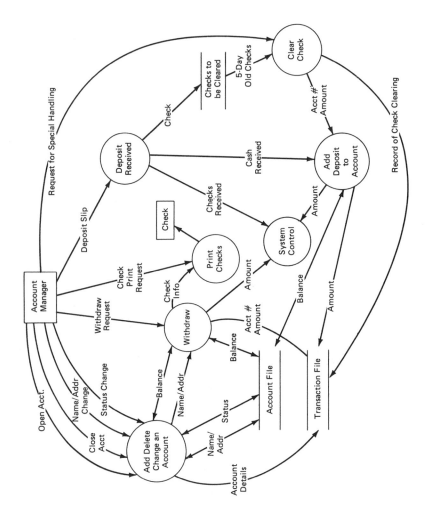

Figure 3–2. Account Betting System Account Management.

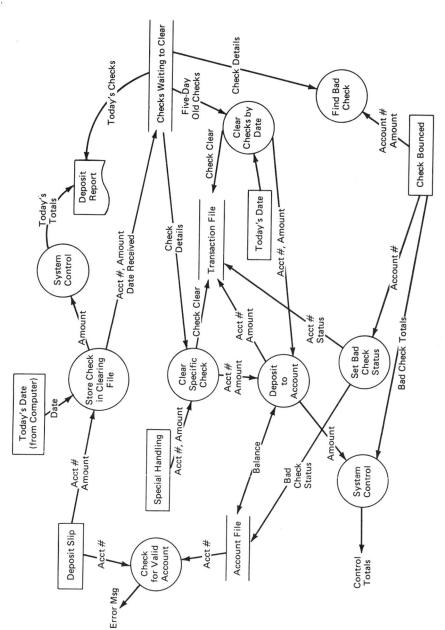

Figure 3-3. Account Betting System Account Management—Check Handling.

streams?" Even my dictionary has the good sense to add a picture. If I said "crocodile" and showed you a picture of a Komodo dragon, "a giant flesh-eating lizard," it's unlikely I would go uncorrected. If I say "payroll system," it brings forth an image of something with hours worked and rates of pay and deductions and paychecks. If I showed you a picture of a payroll system without deductions processing, the fact that something was missing would stand out and the design would be quickly corrected.

There are many ways of setting up a graphic presentation, and the method chosen will have a subtle but significant influence over the life of the project. In our example a series of data flow diagrams was used. The representation of flows and actions was appropriate for a system designed to provide a processing service—the placement of bets for account holders. For a system built to maintain a store of information—for example, an inventory control system—a data-directed presentation such as Warnier-Orr diagrams might be better. For lack of a better term, I would say the form of the presentation should match the "spirit" of the system. When it does, thinking about the system will seem more natural. Mental gear-changes between the idea of the system and the physical picture contained in the presentation materials will be minimized.

It is important the first cut be presented for what it is—a "first cut" at the design. This presentation sets an important tone. It says the design as it stands will be modified and is open to criticism. Since the project leader developed the design and is putting it forth for modification and criticism, he is setting an example for the team: Nobody's designs are sacrosanct. This is a leadership issue and it is important to make the point early. Open design and code review are critical to the success of the crunch-mode project.

Presentation Tools

Remember that you, as the designer of the system, will be *presenting* your ideas and understanding of the system to other people. The effectiveness of the presentation depends upon your ability to communicate your intentions and concerns. This is not the time to deliver masses of technical detail about the capabilities of the hardware or the database system you're thinking of. In fact, if you're tempted to include this sort of material, you've probably been emphasizing the wrong things up to this point.

The first-cut presentation is still concerned with *what the system will do*, not how the system will do it. The tools you use in the presentation should help you communicate your understanding in a way that allows other people to "get inside your head" and understand the way you perceive the system.

Data flow diagrams have been around for several years.[1] A key to their longevity is the way customers and users respond to them. They are, in a word, *non-threatening*. They use terms familiar to the user. They don't contain computer jargon. They have the ability to depict both manual and automated processing in a coherent manner. Since they can be understood by the user without requiring an initial period of study, they make a great tool for presentations.

The designer with a set of data flow diagrams laid out on large posters can lead his audience through the system's processing in a straightforward manner. His audience, even if they have limited exposure to computer systems, can follow the presentation and contribute to it. The designer can break frequently during the presentation to check with the customer and ensure that his understanding of the required processing is correct. Take a look at Figure 3-4 and compare it to Figure 3-3. It shows the changes added during the presentation as a direct result of customer comments. The ability to incorporate changes quickly and easily is exceptionally valuable in a presentation tool.

I have found it useful to combine data flow diagrams and Warnier-Orr[2] diagrams in presentations. The Warnier-Orr diagrams are a nice tool for presenting data organization to the user. A Warnier-Orr diagram of a bet record in the Call-a-Bet system is included as Figure 3-5. Presenting data structures to the user as a hierarchy helps the user and the designer recognize missing elements. The designer may also get a better feeling for the way the user sees the interrelationships between individual items or groups of items.

Even if the eventual implementation will be done with a "relational" database design, I find it useful to represent the data in heirarchical form in the first cut. At this level, the data in the system is going to be viewed as a set of functional groupings, such as an order or a customer history record. This is most likely to be the way the customer thinks of the data. In the next phase of the project, where we will be concerned with the detailed organization of the data, we can decompose the functional groupings to give the system flexibility, if that is what's needed.

Both data flow diagrams and Warnier-Orr diagrams can be created quickly and understood quickly. Each is effective in presenting the system to the customer. Each is effective in forcing some discipline on the early stages of thinking about the system. For the crunch-mode project, it is difficult to recommend other techniques for the first cut.

There has been a lot written recently about automated design aids. There are some excellent ones available, and they can be extremely useful in a crunch-mode project. However, I don't think they are the best tools to use for developing presentation materials. Their real strength can be shown once detailed system design commences and that's where they will be discussed.

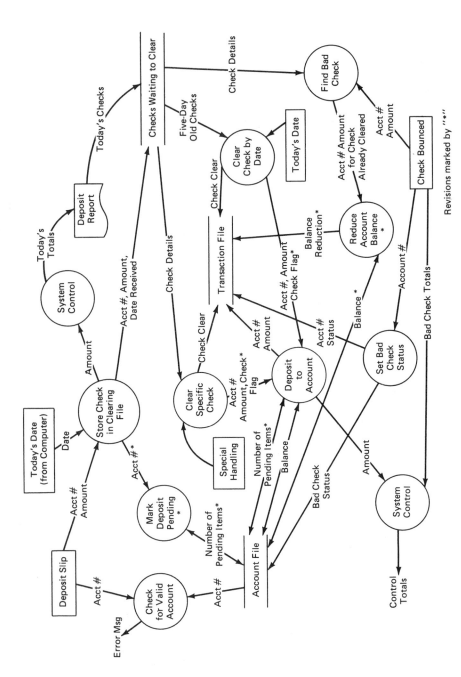

Figure 3-4. Account Betting System Account Management—Check Handling Revised after Presentation.

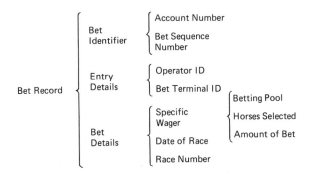

Figure 3-5.   Structure of the Bet Record (This is a Warnier-Orr Diagram).

The Geography of the System

In the process of developing the first cut, the designer will develop a feel for certain features of the system he is going to build. In this, he is much like the explorer who notes where the mountains are and where the rivers run but does not worry about drawing a precise map. The impression of the characteristics of the system to be built will have an enormous effect on the design and implementation strategy adopted for the project.

Perhaps the most important impression is a feel for the "shape" of the system. "System shape" is not an exact description. Figures 3-6 and 3-7 might give you a better idea of the term. The first diagram, Figure 3-6, is an overview of a part of the Call-a-Bet system. It's a wide, loosely-connected system. Figure 3-7 is an overview of the DuPont COMOC® gasoline blending control system. It's a narrow, tightly-connected system.

Generally speaking, wide systems are better prospects for crunch-mode development than narrow systems because they are easier to partition. When you partition a system for development, you look for parts of the system that can be developed in parallel—that is, parts that don't depend upon each other being present in order to function.

Transaction processing systems are usually wide systems. To the extent the transactions involved are independent, development can proceed on several transactions at one time. If progress is slower than expected and it becomes necessary to reduce the scope of the system in order to deliver it on schedule, it may be possible to eliminate one or two less important transactions.

Wide systems often have a fairly small number of interfaces, each of which is used by several functions. In a transaction system, the various transactions affect the contents of common files. The input to a series of functions related to a file (Add a Record, Find a Record, Delete a Record, Update a Record) is likely to have a common input format. Full definition

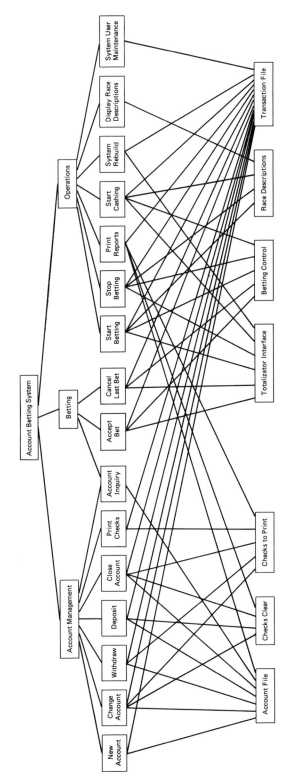

Figure 3-6. Account Betting System Overview of Major File Usage.

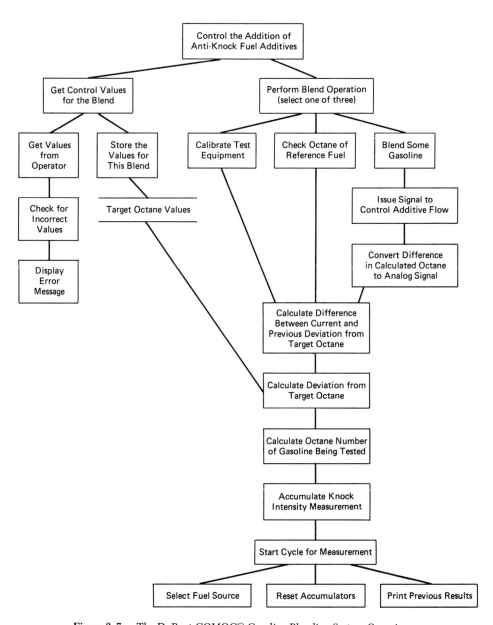

Figure 3-7.   The DuPont COMOC® Gasoline Blending System Overview.

of the interfaces in a wide system can sometimes be delayed until the levels themselves are implemented. Narrow systems, in contrast, may have a variety of interfaces passsing from level to level. The nature of all these interfaces should be understood early in the project.

Please understand that the comments above are generalities. I have found them true often enough to be useful, but they may not be a reliable guide to your next system.

Response and Rework

It is rare that the first cut won't require changes. Just as it did for the designer, the first cut presentation helps the customer organize her thoughts about the system. The most common change is something that was left out either because the designer thought it was a minor issue or because he never suspected it was there.

If the response to the first cut uncovers major misunderstandings or omissions, all the mental alarms should sound. Either the designer doesn't understand the system or the customer has changed her mind about the goals of the system. In neither case should the project proceed until the source of the problem is identified. If the customer honestly believes the misunderstandings are the fault of the designer, she should insist the project be reinitiated with another designer. If both sides agree the requirements have changed, the project might need to be dropped from consideration as a crunch-mode effort.

Remember, it has been only a short time since the project was started. If the purpose of the system has been significantly changed during this short time, it can be expected to change again. It's a mistake to commit significant manpower and money to a project where the primary goals are unclear. The end result is seldom satisfactory, and constant changes that will likely occur during the development period will demoralize and disgust the people who are trying to implement the system.

November 19, 1980

Since the changes to the initial design had been covered during the initial presentation, Ben prepared an updated set of drawings and mailed them to Louisville Downs for approval. He phoned the track's representatives and went over the changes with them. In response to his question, the men at the track said they hadn't thought of anything that wasn't covered in the presentation and the corrections. They felt the system should be built as specified.

Assuming the changes required as a result of the presentation are minor, the presentation material should be changed to reflect them as quickly as possible and the presentation should be given again. This might seem to be a duplication of effort, but in practice it's often valuable. The customer and the project team will have had time to think about the project as presented and may come up with points of concern that they couldn't put their finger on during the initial presentation.

The Project Team and the Presentation

The project can be strengthened by insuring the project team attends the presentation of the first cut and also subsequent presentations where revisions are covered. Members of the team should be encouraged to ask the customer and the project leader questions about the nature and use of the system. There are several benefits to this approach:

• The customer and the project team will actually meet each other in an atmosphere where there is both interest and enthusiasm for the project. Too often, the members of a project team think of the customer as a disembodied entity and the customer thinks of the project team as a group that doesn't particularly appreciate how important the system is to her.

• With the project team in attendance, there are likely to be more questions, including some that stimulate the customer to remember items she may have otherwise overlooked.

• The project team members are able to see themselves as partners in developing the specifications for the system they must build. "Being in on the ground floor" of a system development effort is a situation that fires the imaginations of many programmers and analysts.

• The project leader is showing by example that design is an open process. Design is expected to be made public for comments and criticism. The comments and criticism act to strengthen the design of the system and its parts.

The project leader must act to restrain those members of the team who want to take the presentation down to the level of technical detail. If technical issues are raised at all, they should be at a high level. "Are you sure this hardware has enough power to run the system you're describing?" is a good example of a technical issue that might be raised at the presentation. "Are you thinking of having these processes communicate through a shared memory area?" is an example of a question dealing with a level of detail that should not be a topic of discussion at this point.

The project leader and the team members must remember that the level of discussion during the presentation must not get so esoteric that the customer feels "frozen out." If that happens, the presentation will not accomplish what it should and the project will be off to a rocky start. The project leader can usually control the level of discussion by pointing out that questions or comments related to technical detail are detailed design or implementation issues.

The Importance of "Top-Down" Thinking

In order to present a system as an entity and not just a collection of individual programs, it must be treated in a "top-down" manner. At the highest level there is a statement about the purpose of the system. For example, "The Call-a-Bet system will allow a racetrack to maintain accounts for customers who will place bets over the phone." This is decomposed at lower levels into statements about the parts of the system. They, in turn, are further decomposed into smaller, more specific parts. The top-down approach is inherent in virtually every recognized systems development methodology.

Treating a complex problem by breaking it down into a group of smaller, more manageable problems is an approach taken for granted in most fields of human endeavor. In a crunch-mode development effort, it should be consciously reaffirmed to insure it is not bypassed for a perceived advantage in saving time.

It is particularly important to do this as the project moves from the presentation, which specifies functionality, to design, which specifies structure. I have seen two promising projects fail miserably because the principles of the top-down approach were not applied at this critical point. In both cases, the requirements for the system had just been agreed to by the customer and the designer. But then, in each case, rather than designing the system, the project leaders chose to approach the work to be done by modifying an existing system that had "a number of features analogous to the ones needed in the new system."

Their motivation was understandable. They thought they could start by adapting a system that already included many of the functions they might otherwise need to develop as new programs. They saw this as a great time-saving strategy. It wasn't. Without a top-down design to guide them, evaluation of the existing system was fragmented. The new system included functions it didn't require because they were necessary for the old system it was based on. With no top-down design to serve as the basis for a test plan, system testing became a fiasco.

One of the systems was supposed to be a seven-month project, but it wound up requiring fifteen months, including one aborted installation attempt. I spoke to the project leader after the second installation. She told me she had realized her mistake about three months into the project but felt unable to turn back.

> "I really handled it backward," she said. "If I'd gone ahead and done a detailed design of the new system first, I could have taken stuff out of the other system when I needed it. I was right that there were a lot of programs we could use, but I didn't realize the amount of extra junk we'd have to wade through to get them. Of course, by the time I knew I'd messed up we'd already told the customer that our approach was virtually no-risk because we were basing it on a system that was already in the field. I talked to my boss about the problems and he told me we'd just have to make it work."

On a crunch-mode project there is absolutely no substitute for the top-down approach. This approach must be taken in developing the presentation, in developing the design, in developing the estimates, in designing the individual programs, in developing the test plan—in *everything!* It is the only sensible way to get started quickly and to manage the development once the system starts coming together. It is the only way to reduce the risk of false starts. It is the only approach that gives you the ability to judge the effect of development problems in one area on the rest of the system.

Top-down thinking is too important to be taken for granted!

Chapter 4

SCHEDULES
AND
ESTIMATES

Everyone who comes in here wants three things:
1. They want it quick.
2. They want it good.
3. They want it cheap.
I tell 'em to pick two and call me back.

Sign on the back wall of
a small printing company
in Delaware.

If you are given a project due in ninety days, you may feel scheduling and estimating are both a waste of time. The schedule's been set: Deliver the system in ninety days. Just what are you supposed to estimate? If that's the way you feel, you couldn't be more wrong. Schedules and estimates are critical to the success of a crunch-mode project. If you are doing a good job of managing the project, you'll be spending a fair amount of time on both of them.

You don't believe it? Think about the first estimate you'll be asked to make. "Can you deliver the system on time?" That question will be asked many times during a crunch-mode project. Without schedules and a methodical approach to estimation, you won't be able to answer it. And if you can't answer it with confidence, your project is out of control.

The Fruits of Software Estimating

Software estimation generally has a bad reputation. Projects delivered "on time and within budget" are still the exception in many sectors of the computer industry. Software project managers have developed a real inferiority complex about their ability to estimate. There are more than a few books and articles that decry the state of the art in software estimating.

Much of the bad reputation is a bum rap.

A common example of "good" estimating is construction work. In the construction of single-family homes, delivery of products on schedule is a common occurrence. The quoted price allows the construction company a fair profit because costs are accurately estimated when the job begins. Most of the tasks involved can be looked up in an estimator's handbook and priced with a high degree of confidence.

Just as an experiment, I went to a couple of contractors and asked them what it would cost to build a four-bedroom, brick and frame contemporary house of about 2,800 square feet with a two-car garage, two bathrooms, central air-conditioning, and a patio. They looked at me like I was crazy. Neither one wanted to supply me with any sort of number until he'd seen the architect's plans and the lot where the house would be built and knew about the finishing details. But I perservered, asking for a "rough estimate," a "ballpark" figure, a "general range." It turned out my house could cost anywhere from $90,000 to $260,000.

I don't offer this little experiment as a way of knocking the construction industry, but as a counterpoint to the way of doing business in the world of computer systems. In the construction industry there is a tremendous reluctance to make an estimate, even a casual one, until the job and all the details can be studied. This would be equivalent to a software manager making an estimate after the entire system had been designed through the individual module level. If managers and project leaders had the luxury of waiting until this point to give estimates, you can be sure the quality of the estimates would be greatly improved.

The estimates that come back to haunt project leaders are the early "ballpark" figures. These are most often given to informal inquiries like, "How much do you think it'll take to add group billing to the system?" If the answer is "Oh, probably about four months with three people," the project leader is a marked man. If he actually is directed to do the job and, after the design is complete, announces it will really take six people eight months, nobody is likely to say, "Thanks—we really needed a better estimate." What he's more likely to get is pointed questions as to why the first estimate was for twelve man-months and the second one was for forty-eight. There will be pressure put on him to come up with a third estimate, closer to the first one. Tom DeMarco writes:

> I have sat through sessions in which estimates were haggled as at a bazaar: "Fifteen months." "No more than nine." "I can't do it in less than a year, no matter what." "My final offer is eleven months." "You got it."
>
> I have trouble keeping a straight face at such sessions. But I'm usually the only one; all others are deadly serious. They think what they're doing is "estimating" and probably believe it helps them to hone their abilities. I think of it as low comedy.[1]

The result of this low comedy is not an estimate. It's just a number. Nevertheless, this number is referred to when people who should know better complain about the accuracy of software estimates.

A Different Kind of Estimating

The estimates made during a crunch-mode project are different from those given on other projects. On a typical project, you might be asked how long it will take to build the new system and what manpower will be needed during the development effort. On a crunch-mode project, you are asked the probability that the system will be completed by a given time. These sound like two sides of the same coin, but they aren't.

In the first case you are being asked to set a goal. You say the new system can be ready in thirteen months with a staff of five? That's your goal. You set it. Failure is unthinkable. Even if you went through the negotiation charade described earlier, the "estimate" is yours. Sometimes management is honest enough to refer to estimating along these lines as "goal setting."

In the crunch-mode project, an estimate of the probability of system completion contains an important element not found in the usual estimating process. The possibility of failure is declared. If you say, "There's an eighty percent chance we'll make it by March 1st," you are also saying there's a twenty percent chance you will fail. This acknowledgement of the possibility of failure makes the crunch-mode estimate a true estimate, an opinion about the course of future events that considers more than one outcome.

A number of project managers (me included), hate to estimate in percentages. They imply an accuracy that seldom exists. A close friend of mine was leading a data entry system project. When he attended the company's quarterly project review meeting, he got involved in the following exchange with the executive vice-president:

> "Where does the new data entry project stand?"
> "Well, sir, we've recovered from the initial hardware delays and things are generally on schedule."
> "Can you be more specific?"
> "We've met the last two milestones and there shouldn't be a problem with the in-house demo next week."
> "Fine, but where do we stand on completing the project?"
> "Are you looking for a percentage of completion or something like that?"
> "That's exactly what I need."

"Oh, OK. Hmmm. Just a second. Hmmm. OK. We're 68.5 percent complete at this point."
"Good."

Incredible!

To avoid the percentage trap, particularly early in the project, an estimate might take the following form.

> The automatic teller functions and the audio response system can be in place by July 15th. You might be able to squeeze in the bookkeeping update functions but it would be tight. If you want to try for the linkup to the credit card verification network, that's a little more effort than the bookkeeping update. I don't think there's any way to include the interbank transfers and meet the schedule.

The form of the estimate should be influenced by the nature of the project. If the system to be produced has been reduced to its essentials, estimates in the form of a probability of project completion are most suitable, even if they are not quantified to tenths of a percent. If there is a possibility of a phased implementation, estimates reflecting the impact of individual functional areas on delivery by a given date will be more informative.

November 30, 1980

The Call-a-Bet system was reduced to its essentials as part of the presentation development. Both the customer and Ben's management wanted to know if delivery by February 15th was possible. Ben's only statement at the time of the presentation was that delivery would be a really tight squeeze. He told the customer he would have better estimates in another week to ten days and he urged them to think about a "drop-dead date." This would be the date when they would need to know if the system could not be delivered on the original schedule.

Ben knew Louisville Downs and Dynatote would need to take certain action, probably both operational and legal, if the system couldn't be delivered on schedule. These steps would take time and they would need to be taken before racing began at the track.

In order to develop the better estimates he had promised, Ben needed to move from the functional description of the system embodied in the presentation to a representation related to the actual work to be performed. He needed to identify not only specific tasks but interrelationships between tasks. He needed a road map from where he was now to the point where the system was finished.

Estimates given this way do the job estimates are supposed to do. They guide the customer and your management in making decisions about the project as a whole. If your estimate of the chances of finishing the project by the date set are lower than the customer's "threshold of acceptable risk," the customer will be faced with a decision. Should the scope of the system be modified? Should the delivery date be changed? Should more resources be added to the project? Your estimate has put everybody on notice that the project as it stands is in trouble.

The Development Road Map

The schedule is the road map. A schedule is really nothing more than a plan with time estimates included. It is a statement by the project leader about his intention to perform tasks in a certain order and his expectation they will be completed in a specified time.

Crunch-mode schedules are both similar and different from schedules for "normal" projects. Take a look at Figures 4-1(a) and 4-1(b). They are similar in the way they both address the set of tasks that must be performed to build *any* decent software. They are different in the way they reflect the order in which the tasks are carried out. In the crunch-mode project there will almost always be a high degree of overlap among design and imple-

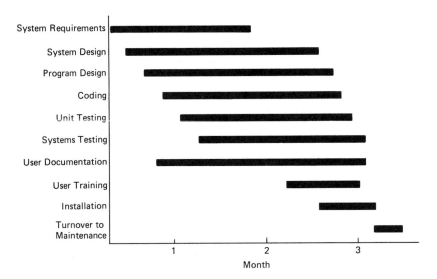

Figure 4-1 (a).   A Typical Crunch-Mode Schedule.

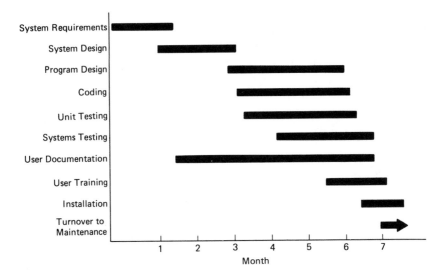

Figure 4-1 (b).   A Normal Project Schedule.

mentation activity. In normal system activity, a good manager will take the time to do more design up front, before committing resources to implementation.

What goes into the schedule? How do we make the jump from presentation materials to pieces of the system? We need to have an abstraction of the programs to be written in order to estimate the effort involved in actual development of the software and to set up the schedule. Furthermore, in the crunch-mode project we need to have the abstraction quickly.

For years the jump from specification to design was regarded as something occult, the result of a magical art vouchsafed to a chosen few. This is no longer the case. If you understand what the system is to do, identifying the specific procedures needed is almost mechanical. Some recent developments provide automated support and verification of the design.

The approach Ben chose to get from the presentation to a design was a brute-force approach. He started at the top and went down until he got to modules that had a specific purpose or handled only one condition. The process didn't take very long: The diagrams were finished in about four and a half days. Because the brute-force approach makes all design decisions "local," most complex design decisions are avoided.

A local design decision deals strictly with a module and its immediate subordinates. It assumes all data necessary for the modules to carry out their work is available. Local design decisions are the lifeblood of "functional decomposition." If there is an art to the process, it is in not rushing to detail too quickly. The use of a graphic abstraction like the diagrams in the

December 1, 1980

Ben started the design of the Call-a-Bet system by drawing a single box:

He realized the key to successful top-down design is starting at the top. The next step followed quickly:

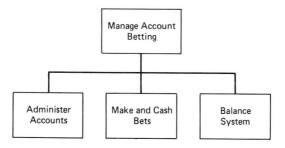

Including the Balance System module at this level was done simply because Ben had experience in developing racetrack systems. Financial controls in the racing industry are extremely tight. Regulatory and tax authorities usually have personnel on site to guard the integrity of the operation and ensure taxes are promptly collected. The concept of a system with controls "added on"—rather than "designed in"—didn't occur to Ben.

While Ben was developing his road map, he made no attempt to identify specific information to be passed between modules and he made no attempt to consolidate his modules. Every module had a unique path back to the top level. The idea was to identify all the pieces necessary to perform a particular task.

As you can imagine, the final drawing was very large. Actually, it was a collection of drawings using the same oversized posterboard stock Ben used in the presentation. The large format made it possible to lay out all the required modules for a major function in one or two drawings. A "major" function was any user-initiated transaction, such as opening a new account. The diagrams used for the Close Account function are shown in Figure 4-2.

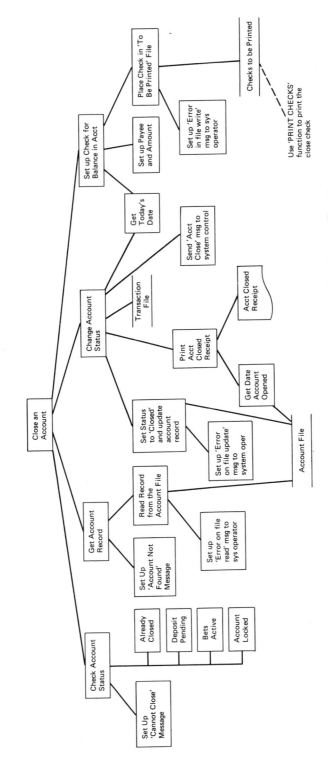

Figure 4-2. Account Betting System Account Management—Close Account Function.

examples is a help in avoiding too much detail too soon. While the diagrams do not give a true tree structure, they get very unwieldy if they spread out too quickly. A diagram that's difficult to handle is not necessarily wrong: a program that handles twenty individual transaction types *is* going to spread out. But if you have a diagram that looks unbalanced or one that has to be squeezed to make it fit on paper, you should take a second look at it to see if you've bypassed some reasonable intermediate-level modules.

December 6, 1980

When Ben looked at the final set of diagrams, he knew he'd need to do a little more work to make them suitable as a basis for estimates. The way they stood, he had about forty boxes that said "Get Account." Clearly there was no way he was going to write forty Get Account procedures.

By looking through the diagrams, Ben was able to identify a number of "bottom-level" boxes used over and over in the diagrams. These were grouped together as likely candidates for a procedure library. If there was a question as to whether a particular module was general enough for inclusion in the library, Ben left it out. [Figure 4-3 shows the effect of identifying library procedures on the Close Account function. The amount of unique code needed for the function is reduced substantially.] Ben also started to get a feel for the testing environment and began to lay out a set of modules needed for development and testing. These modules would constititute a library of development and installation tools.

Once the library membership had been set up, it was time for a very quick design review. Ben made sure Barbara, the junior programmer assigned to the project, took part in the review. The module drawings were not intended for a presentation to the customer—they were strictly for the project team.

The review compared the module drawings to the data flow charts and looked for completeness. If the design was complete, it would be possible to identify groups of modules corresponding to functions in the data flow diagram. Ben and Barbara were specifically looking for three conditions that indicate incompleteness.

1. Any function in the data flow diagram which didn't have a corresponding group of boxes in the module drawing.

2. Any function in the data flow diagram where the function appeared to be supported by boxes in the module drawing which weren't grouped together.

3. Any set of boxes in the module drawing without a corresponding function in the data flow diagrams.

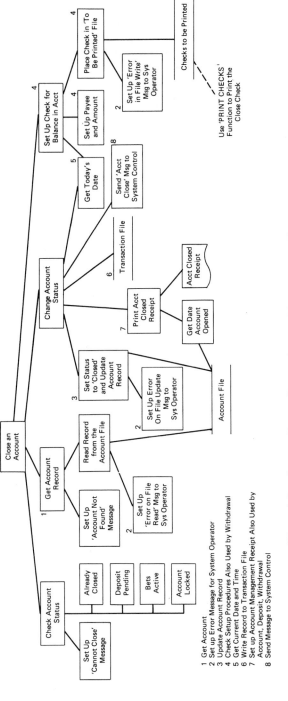

Figure 4-3. Account Betting System Account Management—Close Account Function Library Procedures Indicated.

52

Figure 4-4 shows the data flow diagram for the Close Account function. Are the above conditions met?

Although I refer to the boxes in the diagrams as "modules," they are
not modules in the sense of representing specific program units. At this time
no "packaging" has taken place. Looking at the diagrams, it is possible to
determine actions the computer will perform, but it isn't clear how many
programs will be written.

How do you know when the level of detail in the module drawings is
sufficient? The project manager's only guide is experience. Not only his experience, but the experience of other senior people on the team. When the
project manager puts a box into the module drawings, he will have an idea
of the amount of complexity and code the box represents. For modules in
the upper levels of the design, the idea will be fairly vague. As the design
goes to lower levels, modules that look familiar will appear. They might
have names like "Get Account Record" or "Calculate FICA Withholding."
The experienced programmer has written or looked at modules that do
things very similar to the ones that now appear in the design. He knows
they will take a page of code, or a half-page or a page and a half. The exact
amount of code isn't as important as the designer's knowledge that he has
seen code like this and knows the amount of effort it takes to produce it.

The third condition Ben and Barbara were looking for might seem a
little unusual. But the fact is, thinking about the system and what it needs
to do does not stop with the presentation. Although the presentation materials are referenced in developing the module drawings, the drawings are
not a simple re-drawing of the presentation materials.

It's as if we were describing a community with two maps. The first is
a topographic map showing the land and its natural features. The second is
a road map showing buildings and other man-made objects. When we look
at them both we can see they complement each other, but we can also see
how each has influenced the other. The top of this hill has been leveled to
allow an airplane landing strip to be put in. The road over there curves to
avoid the patch of sandy ground.

It's the same with the presentation and the module drawings. They
work in concert to describe the same system and they also influence each
other. In many cases control and housekeeping functions that were overlooked in setting up the presentation become clear as specific sets of procedures are defined. If the module drawings show omissions in the presentation material, the presentation material should be updated.

Interlude

Where are we now? In the project we are following, Ben has developed a set of presentation materials and a group of module drawings. The

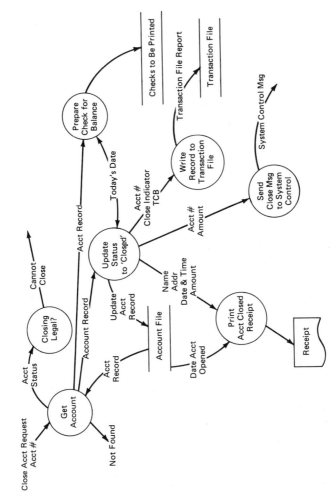

Figure 4-4. Account Betting System Account Management—Close Account Function DFD.

presentation materials were used to define the functions of the system. The module drawings will be used to develop a strategy for building the system and also as a basis for estimates.

The module drawings as presented here do not fit into any well-known methodology. They do not constitute a formal design. What they are is an estimate of the design, done in the expectation that a rigorous top-down design effort would yield a similar system. They will be used to develop estimates of the effort required to build the system. Because we are looking at a crunch-mode project, we are sacrificing some accuracy to get a quick result.

Despite the lessened accuracy, the project leader should have confidence in estimates drawn from these materials. It is unlikely any piece of the system requiring substantial additional effort will appear unless the scope of the system changes. Just by looking at the drawings, the project leader should be able to form an opinion about the relative complexity of different functions within the system. Last, but by no means least, going through the effort of developing module drawings will make it difficult for the project leader to deceive himself about the amount of work to be done.

Sink or Swim

Knowing the work to be done is not enough to develop a decent set of estimates. How long would it take you to split a cord of seasoned oak into reasonably sized pieces for the fireplace? If you're out of shape and only have a dull hatchet to work with it will take you longer than it would if you were in excellent physical condition and used a splitting maul. A reasonable estimate will take into account the resources to do the work as well as the work itself.

The project leader needs to take an inventory of his resources before he gives an estimate. If lack of resources will prevent the job from scheduled completion, he must be prepared to identify the additional resources needed. Resources come in a number of forms.

People. This is usually the critical resource. The project leader must pay attention to the quality of the people as well as the number. We know the ability of programmers varies widely.[2] The project leader must try to identify the number of "very good to excellent" programmers he can call on. These will be the people who carry the project. If specific skills are needed (a person who knows about the database package to be used, or someone who is familiar with a specific communications protocol), the project leader must be sure he can get a qualified person on the team.

December 1, 1980

When Ben and Barbara had finished the design review, Ben looked up and said, "The two of us stand absolutely no chance of getting this thing up and running on time." At that point, he realized delivery would depend on getting the people he needed on the team quickly. The estimating process would need to give him an idea of the resources he needed, and this would become a factor in estimating the probability of on-time delivery.

Machine availability.   How quickly will the job get done if you can only get on the system to test between noon Saturday and 6 a.m. Monday? On a crunch-mode development project, system use starts early in the project and continues at a high level throughout. The recent developments in automated design and programming aids increase the need for hardware availability. Bluntly speaking, you can't get too much of it. One company I know provides each of its programmers with two terminals: One is used for running the application and the other is used for debugging it. Both tie into a system used only for application development. Individual programmer productivity during program testing has gone up by as much as twenty percent when measured in time to complete a system module.

Hardware availability is a real problem if your project is using prototype equipment. In this case there's very little you can do except add a "fudge factor" to allow for the effects of hardware that either doesn't work or undergoes changes that make it necessary to change already-written software to accommodate it. When you give your estimates, make sure the fudge factor is explicitly identified.

December 10, 1980

Except for people, Ben couldn't really complain about development resources. The team would have a dedicated set of computers located at a nearby racetrack. The track was closed during the winter, so interruptions would be at a minimum. Office space was tight but sufficient. None of the equipment was prototype equipment. The operating system had a few idiosyncrasies, but they were well known.

The computer manufacturer had recently announced the availability of Pascal on the system. The other languages available were Assembler, FORTRAN and APL. A 'C' compiler was in the works. Ben chose to use Pascal for the system; it turned out to have some benefits he hadn't foreseen.

System tools.   What tools can your programmers use to get the most from their time? What languages are available? Are there prototyping tools or program generators? What's the database system like? There is a pile of questions in this area, and the answers each affect how long it will take to get the job done.

If you know of tools that aren't installed on the system you'll be using, make an effort to get them. Don't be shy about getting something you know only by reputation. If it looks like it will speed up the development process, get it and look at it in person.

Avoiding Compromise

If you look at the resources, the job to be done, and the date the system is to be delivered and come to the conclusion the combination simply won't work, say so now. You don't need to wait to develop detailed estimates about the extra resources or time you will need. As the person responsible for the project, it's your responsibility to make sure the bad news gets back to the people who can deal with it. If they ask what extra resources or time is required, tell them you'll have some details once the estimates are finished.

If you feel a particular piece of hardware or a person with specific expertise is required for the project to have any chance of success, say so. Make sure it's clear to your management that the additional resource doesn't guarantee success, but its absence makes failure very likely.

There's no point in compromising on the things you feel you really need. After all, you are the one who is carrying responsibility for the project, and at this point you know more about it than anyone else.

You may get some searching questions about the things you want. This is to be expected. Even before you come out with your estimates, the customer and your management will have a mental picture of the complexity and cost of the system. Your requests will raise that cost and may force reevaluation of the original business decision. If your management asks you to say exactly how much will be gained if you get that multiple communication procotol analyzer you're asking for, the answer need not be an absolute number:

> The multi-protocol analyzer lets us set up error conditions in the protocol directly on the line rather than writing another program to simulate network errors. Setup time for individual tests will be cut at least in half because we can use the switches on the tester to change conditions instead of loading another program or changing file configurations. We're going to be running literally hundreds of test cases as we go toward installation.

Don't ask for a lot of extra resources as a ploy to "cover your tail," planning to blame their absence if the project is late. It's dishonest, and your management will see right through it.

Milestones and Tombstones

Crunch-mode projects live and die by their milestones. A milestone event is an event that must occur if the project is to be completed. The combination of the event and the date it should occur comprise a milestone. Milestones need to be meaningful and they need to be set up early. When a milestone event occurs on or before it is scheduled, you have "made the milestone." When it doesn't occur until after the scheduled date has passed, the milestone was "missed." If you make all the milestones, the project will finish on time. If you miss one, the chance you won't complete the project on schedule grows.

Milestones must be tied to completion of significant functions. There shouldn't be too many milestones in a short period of time. If you see more than one milestone occurring in a five-day period, check to see if you can't remove one from your proposed list. A milestone does not occur whenever a module or function is completed. In fact, it typically takes dozens of programs working together to complete a significant function.

This means that before you set milestones, you must figure out how long it will take you to develop the underlying programs and get them working as a unit. It's finally time to do the estimates.

Some Estimating Heuristics

How do you estimate how long it will take someone else to develop a program? How good are you in estimating how long it will take *you* to develop a program? Estimating techniques come in a lot of flavors in the software world. Some work well on one project and fall apart on another. Some work well for one person and not for another. What follows is a list of ideas and approaches dealing with the process of estimating software projects. These heuristics should be regarded as tools to be used in developing the initial estimate. Subsequent estimates can be tempered by empirical data gathered from the performance of the project team.

• "For some years I have been successfully using the following rule of thumb for scheduling a software task:

$1/3$ planning
$1/6$ coding
$1/4$ component test and early system test
$1/4$ system test, all components in hand."[3]

It may be easier to go through the module charts and estimate how long it would take to design each piece and then extrapolate than it is to think about all the coding and testing involved. If you are building an enhancement to an existing system, use a ratio more heavily biased toward testing because you need to test more than just your part of the finished product.

• If you have any program estimated for less than a day, round it up to a day.

• When you've completed estimating all the pieces, add five percent for each level of the system, based on your module charts.

• After you've developed a set of estimates, put them away. Go sleep on it and come back in the morning and, without referring to your previous estimates, develop a new set. If they're wildly different, sleep on it and try again tomorrow. Then take the average and use that for your estimate.

• Use a couple of different estimating techniques. If the difference is less than fifteen percent, use the higher one.

• If you have experienced people on the team, get them to give you estimates of pieces of the system *anonymously*. Anonymous estimates are less likely to include extra "safety factors" added when people are asked, "How long would it take *you* to do this?"

• "Estimate by committee. . . . Throw away the estimate by the person directly responsible for the effort. Average the others."[4]

• Simplify. Put every routine into one of three classes: easy, normal, or hard. Assign one day for easy routines, three for normal ones, six for hard, and add things up. If you have pieces that you think will take more than six days, break them down into smaller ones.

In the final analysis, you are estimating from your own experience and from the experience of others. To the extent your module drawings break down into simple pieces that might be found in any system, putting numbers on them becomes easier. As you go into areas where you have no prior experience, the numbers will get higher.

If you are working with an organization that has developed software metrics,[5] don't use any heuristics! Use the available data. That's what it's there for. If your system has some features that are unique, such as a new computer system or a different language, you may need to adjust the metrics to allow for a learning curve. Even if you need to do this, it is much,

much better to base your estimates on recorded performance within your organization than to base them on your own subjective opinions.

Dive and Surface

Once you have your numbers, go back into your module drawings. What you're looking for are some milestones.

December 12, 1980

Ben selected only a few milestones for the Call-a-Bet project. Each of the events could be demonstrated to the customer and to management without interrupting the flow of development activity.

1. Functions for creating an account and making a deposit completed.
2. Functions for processing a telephone bet and sending it to the totalizator completed.
3. Functions for cashing winning tickets at the totalizator and allowing account withdrawals completed.
4. All account management functions completed.
5. Telephone operator and operator supervisor functions completed.
6. Computer operations room functions completed.
7. System restart validated.
8. Start of installation.

Each function involved not only the function initialization and response, but also the associated system controls and reporting processes to show the function had taken place correctly. In many cases, the function being demonstrated was supported by "stubs," but the programs that made up the function being shown were actual production programs. [Figure 4-5 shows the modules required for completion of the first milestone.]

At this time, Ben had still not packaged the modules in his drawing into programs. He felt the packaging could be worked out later with the individual programmers.

Because the Call-a-Bet system dealt with a variety of independent transactions, Ben was able to look at it as a collection of individual projects connected by the file system and the system control functions. It seemed more reasonable to him to go in and develop a complete individual function before moving to the next than to try to make progress on all functions simultaneously.

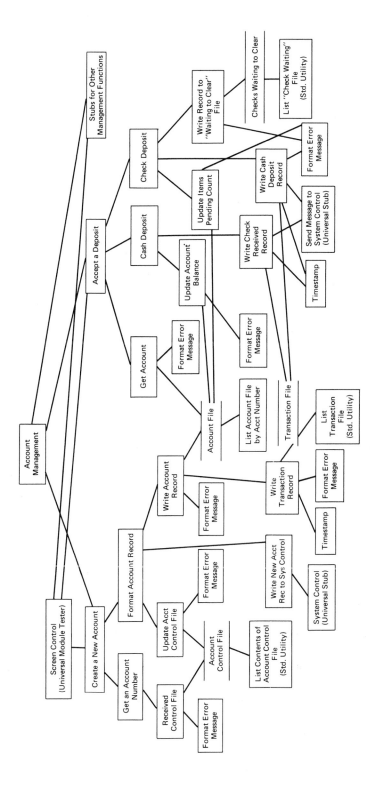

Figure 4-5. Account Betting System—First Milestone Required Programs.

For a system combining several independent functions, this dive-and-surface approach is a good one for several reasons.

- Tools and test data developed for the first function will find use in the other functions to be developed.
- Interfaces at several levels of the system will be tested at an early point in the project. If there are problems, they will come to light before they affect substantial numbers of programs.
- The project team will gain confidence as they see the system actually starting to do something useful.
- The project will get to a milestone event more quickly and you can use the experience in adjusting the remaining estimates.

These benefits are substantial, and you should try to obtain them if you can. Although the dive-and-surface approach is most easily defined in a transaction-driven system, variations of the theme can be developed to apply to other system forms. A large-scale data collection and control system might first attempt to get data from one source all the way through the system while treating other data sources as constants.

Ignoring the Budget

It's tough enough setting up a crunch-mode project so it can be delivered on time. If you also need to contend with budget constraints, the job becomes thankless indeed. The best thing you can do is ignore the budget.

Not literally, of course. But you should try to arrange it so it doesn't take any of your time. Asking for someone from the controller's department to help you in this area is a good idea. You can hand over the numbers you came up with in estimating the time required and let your borrowed assistant plug in the unit costs to come up with a total. Since the controller's department will see the actual costs as they are incurred, they can do all the work required to project the spending rate and compare actuals to the original estimates.

If the costs are going well beyond what was allocated, have no fear. The controller will get wind of it and sound the alarm to your management. Only at this point will you be asked to explain what's going on. An involved defense of line items is seldom necessary. Surprising as it seems, it's more difficult to squander money on a crunch-mode project than on one with lots of available time. Since the team is working at a high rate of productivity, the project will probably be using all the allocated resources. If your management wants to reduce spending, you should be able to demonstrate how cutting back on resources may reduce the chances of scheduled delivery.

January 19, 1981

In mid-January, Ben was called in to discuss the rate at which the Call-a-Bet project was consuming money. By referring to the milestones, Ben was able to show the rate would be reduced by the third week in January as two of the programmers would be finished and ready for assignments outside the project. The spending rate would then stay even until the start of the installation.

Even as these discussions were taking place, Ben didn't inquire what the spending rate was. As far as he was concerned, it was the cost of getting substantial production. Neither he nor his management were able to locate any areas of waste.

At the end of the project, Ben still didn't know what the Call-a-Bet system had cost. It was a secondary issue as far as the project management strategy went. The main goal was scheduled delivery.

A Look Backward at the Scheduling Process

It's important to notice at this point what *hasn't* been done on the Call-a-Bet project. An involved PERT chart has not been developed. A detailed project management system has not been set up. A full, detailed design has not been created.

These things haven't been done because there is no time to do them correctly. In a crunch-mode development effort, the pressure of time is inexorable. In a ninety-day project, an estimate available in ten days with accuracy of plus or minus twenty-five percent is a better thing to have than one that's accurate within ten percent but isn't available for another thirty days.

The important benefit of the schedule produced, rough as it may be, is the insight it gives the project leader about the task he faces. If he has approached the development of the schedule in a methodical and consistent manner, he can speak about the possibility of success with confidence. He can request additional resources with a clear idea of how they will be used.

It sometimes happens that he can see the handwriting on the wall. There is such a thing as an impossible deadline. It doesn't need to be outrageous. A development effort that is going to take six months simply will not mesh with a five-month delivery schedule. One month doesn't sound like much until you consider the project is already as tight as it can be and there's no place to make up the extra work.

The scheduling and estimating process is critical because it broadens the project leader's understanding of the system and the way it will be built. It is this system understanding that must be passed on to the programmers who will actually build the system. If the understanding does not exist or if it cannot be communicated, the project will invariably fail.

Chapter 5

PROGRAMMING UNDER PRESSURE

Inventing is a combination of brains and materials. The more brains you use, the less material you need.

Charles F. Kettering

Success in a crunch-mode development project is a direct outcome of the design process. There is simply not enough time to improve a second-rate design as part of the implementation process.

What is sought is *elegance.* Elegance in system design, like elegance in mathematical proofs, gives a deceptive appearance of simplicity. Steve Wozniak's disk controller for the Apple II is elegant. The pipe facility in Unix is elegant. The RSA public-key data encryption scheme is elegant. Elegance at this level is difficult to achieve but worth keeping in mind.

Elegance seldom springs unbidden into the mind of the designer. It is suggested by the system and its requirements. It is nurtured by tools and abstractions that allow a view of the project from many angles. It is an aesthetically pleasing solution to a specific problem posed by the system requirements.

Almost without exception, successful crunch-mode projects contain at least one elegant feature. The feature is usually created during the time when implementation is just getting started and its influence is felt throughout the development period. The leader of a crunch-mode project must concern herself with creating an environment where elegance can come to light.

Foundation Stones

In putting together the presentation and the schedules, there has been no mention of producing lengthy text documentation. The following example should explain why this is so.

Here is some text:

> The knot is composed of three wraps situated one below the other along the axis of the post. The wraps enclose a segment of rope used to form the knot, which lies parallel to the axis of the post. This segment loops around the bottom wrap and ascends vertically on the outside of the wraps to form the beginning of the top wrap.[1]

Here is a picture:

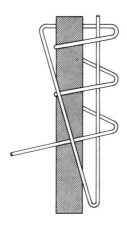

Which of these gave you the better information? Which was more quickly understandable?

Crunch-mode projects, not only in the computer industry but in other branches of engineering, have used pictures in place of words for years. Not only are pictures able to communicate ideas faster than words, they are less subject to misinterpretation. A good crunch-mode project should have very little material that is textual rather than graphic. The only exceptions that come quickly to mind are comments in the code itself and portions of the user manuals.

We have already discussed data flow diagrams and module drawings. Those are the tools that have brought us to this point. We have a specification and an estimate of the design. The project needs to move forward.

December 14, 1980

Once the schedule had been drawn up, Ben turned his attention to the actual implementation of the system. He made up a little list of external features.

The transactions the system was to process would come from operator terminals.

Any given transaction would be independent of the preceding one.

The functions available to an operator would depend on the operator's responsibilities at the racetrack.

Terminals used by different types of operators would be located in different physical areas of the racetrack.

The most frequent transaction would be betting. Since the operator needed to hold an involved conversation with the bettor, transaction rates were likely to be moderate.

Ben took the time to draw up a physical diagram of the system for his own purposes. In the end, it turned out that the diagram wasn't particularly useful for anything but introducing the system to new members of the team. [Since you are being introduced to the system as well, the diagram is included for you as Figure 5-1.]

The substantial benefit of thinking about the physical layout of the system was Ben's decision to let the program organization reflect the physical environment. This was not a radical departure from the design work that had been done to date; it was more an affirmation.

Each operator terminal would be served by a single program that would "own" the terminal. No other program in the system could directly access the terminal. The program would know which type of terminal it was controlling (telephone bet terminal, account supervisor terminal, or another type). For any terminal type, certain transactions were allowed and others were not. For any terminal type, certain operators could "sign on" and others could not.

During the development of the presentation and the schedule, the project leader and other members of the team will have thought about the way the system will be implemented. This is only natural. In dealing with a system that must run on a set of real hardware, approaches to design will be evaluated with the computer and its operating system as a consideration. A reasonable designer doesn't waste time thinking about a graphics-based operator interface for a computer system that doesn't support graphics.

At this point the project needs a high-level software architecture drawing. Let's call it a blueprint. The blueprint deals with actual software

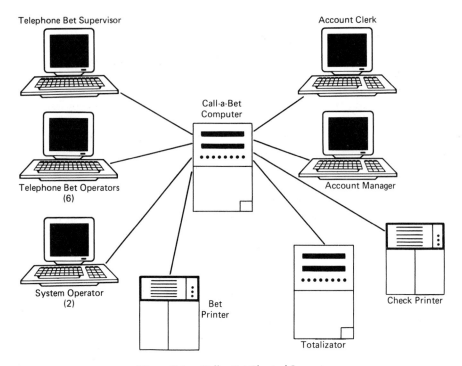

Figure 5–1. Call-a-Bet Physical Layout.

December 16, 1980

Ben took a two-pronged approach to develop the first packaging plan. He didn't spend a great deal of time on it because he realized packaging is one of the most volatile areas of design. The actual packaging would be worked out with the individual programmers as the code was being developed. One prong of the approach was to lay out major functions as individual programs and show their relationship to the terminal programs. This was the blueprint [Figure 5-2].

The second prong of the approach was to see how amenable the module drawings were to a packaging effort. This involved grouping one or more directly connected modules into a possible "program." All the modules in a "program" had to be directly connected to their superordinates. There could not be any "lonely" programs. It was a great relief to find the module drawings came together into "programs" easily.

entities. It is the first step in packaging the software. "Packaging" is the grouping of functions into the individual programs that make up the system.

If the module drawings are developed using local design decisions, there shouldn't be any "lonely" programs. Each module should have a clear and logical connection to the module above it in the drawings.

A Brief Discourse on Method

There are at least two reasonable ways of approaching a system design effort. One is to pick a methodology and its associated design tools and proceed to work through the design. It's not particularly important that you find the "best" technique. Most of the well-known methods can yield good results with a variety of systems when they are properly and consistently applied. If you decide to proceed this way, be sure the technique you've chosen doesn't require you to do a great deal of detailed writing and drawing. You won't have time to do it.

A second way is to get a "fix" on the final system by using several different techniques. Design technique has a subtle effect on the designer's view of the system. Warnier-Orr methods force the designer into dealing with the system as a hierarchy. Yourdon-Constantine structured design leads to looking at lower-level consolidation, or "fan in." If both methods are used, the designer may come away with insights that would be unavailable if she had stuck to a single method.

If possible, the use of more than one design technique should be tried. The amount of time available for system design, no matter what technique is used, is very limited. Within this time, the project leader must get to the point where she is confident the design will be adequate to do the job. Using more than one design technique allows her to check her design. It may not pick up all the detailed problems, but if there are substantial shortcomings in the original design, the use of a second design technique should allow the project leader to spot them.

> Consider your problem from various sides. Emphasize different parts, examine different details, examine the same details repeatedly, approach them from different sides. Try to see some new meaning in each detail, some new interpretation of the whole.
>
> Seek contacts with your formerly acquired knowledge. Try to think of what helped you in similar situations in the past. Try to recognize something familiar in what you examine, try to perceive something useful in what you recognize.[2]

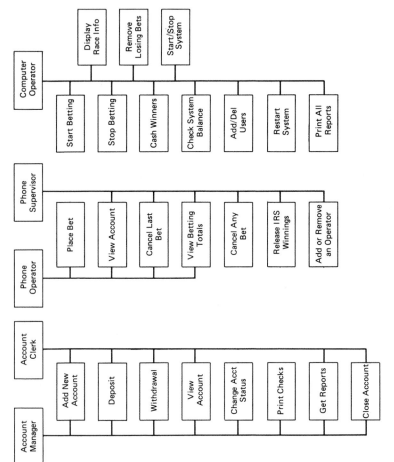

Figure 5-2. Account Betting System Functions by Operator Type (System Blueprint).

In crunch-mode developments such as the Call-a-Bet system, the majority of the design work is done by programmers when they are ready to develop individual programs. With a system made up of several discrete processing paths, there should be few problems if the individuals are properly managed. In a system where a number of processes must work together within the confines of a single path to produce the desired result, leaving design decisions to programmers assigned to the different processes can cause tremendous problems. For this case, the design of the individual processes and their interrelationships must be worked out with the programming team before any coding is begun.

In both cases, there must be an effort to reduce the variety of interfaces as much as possible. The number of files must be reduced to the minimum required. The number of different interprocess messages must also be held as low as possible. Reducing the variety of interfaces reduces the complexity of the implemented system, and this is important. Complexity is the mortal enemy of timely completion. It takes longer to code a complex system than a simple one; it takes *much* longer to test it. It's more difficult to make changes to a complex system.

The crunch-mode system designer's most valuable tool dates from the early part of the fourteenth century—

Entities are not to be multiplied beyond necessity.

William of Ockham

This is known as "Ockham's Razor." It's not used often enough in system design. It is surprising how the critical attitude brought to evaluation of system requirements can slip away as the actual building of the system commences. This is probably a matter of familiarity. When a project leader works on the data flow diagrams and data structures that make up the specifications, she may be walking on ground that is foreign to her. She may not have complete control over her environment—the final say belongs to the customer or to her own management.

Once the system gets to the point where it will be actually built, the project leader and her team will feel more comfortable. They are now ready to write programs. That's something they know how to do. A programmer working on a particular piece of code will often develop "tunnel vision." He will see the problems immediately facing him and will want to take steps to make his own work easier. Many times, the side-effects of these changes are not fully thought out. As a result, the time saved now is paid back later, often at significantly higher cost.

It's not enough for the project leader and her design group to make it simple. There's a considerable amount of work involved in keeping it simple.

Data Dictionaries

The project leader should not spend too much time designing the process architecture. From the limited time available for design, a significant part must be devoted to developing the data architecture. A data dictionary must be started before programming gets underway. The dictionary must contain, as a minimum, descriptions of the information in data files and in interprocess messages.

Most computers have available a data dictionary/database system that can generate data definition statements for inclusion in programs. Many of these systems are also tied to report generators. If you find your development system doesn't include one of these packages, try to purchase one immediately. If such a package is not available for your development system, take time to develop a set of operating procedures to ensure that data definitions can only be updated by one person. Open access to updating the data dictionary is a recipe for confusion.

December 19, 1980

Development of the data dictionary led Ben to the feature of the system he would later describe as "not really 'elegant,' but very nice nonetheless."

As he was defining the interprocess messages, he noticed most of them contained similar information. It was necessary to carry the information from the top level, where it was entered by an operator, to lower levels of the system, where it would be written to files.

The critical file was originally envisioned as a bet file, but it was expanded to become a file to record all system transactions. The expansion was necessary to allow system recovery. To rebuild the system from its start-of-day position, each completed transaction would require reprocessing. Each completed transaction needed, therefore, information about where it was performed, the operator who performed it, the account it affected, and the exact details of the transaction itself.

It struck Ben that a single message format could probably be used throughout the system. He tentatively named the format the Transaction Control Block (TCB) and began to lay it out. He noticed information in the control block would be present for different periods. Since each top-level program would be assigned to a single terminal, the terminal information for that program's Transaction Control Block would stay constant. Once an operator had signed on, information identifying him would be moved to the message and it would stay there until he signed off. A single account might be used for several transactions: Bets on three different races would generate three different transactions. The individual transaction information was the shortest-lived element in the TCB.

Ben set up the block by concatenating the operator record, the terminal record, the account record, and the transaction record as he had them laid out. The Transaction Control Block would carry a "pass/fail" item to inform the higher-level process if the lower-level one had been successful. Ben also decided to include the screen image in the TCB. This let lower-level processes set up error and advisory messages directly.

Once he convinced himself the approach would work, Ben sat down with Barbara, his junior programmer. He explained the function of the Transaction Control Block and told Barbara he wanted to have a Universal Module Tester developed. The two of them worked out a program design [see Figures 5-3 and 5-4] and Barbara got started on the coding.

The Universal Module Tester would allow an operator to interactively set values in a Transaction Control Block, send the TCB to the process being tested and display the contents when the called process returned the block at completion of its task. A slightly modified version of the tester would be used as the Universal Stub, taking the place of lower-level processes that were not yet developed during both module and system testing. Since all processes used the TCB for communication with other processes, these would be the only two test programs required. The interactive nature of the module testers allowed programmers to set up a wide variety of conditions quickly.

The concept was, as Ben described it, "very nice." It meant a tremendous saving of time for the programmers since they would not need to develop "test beds" for individual module testing. Further, the limited signalling allowed between processes kept the system free of "pathological linkages."[3] Also, the presence of the Transaction Control Block acted as a check against added complexity at lower levels.

The Transaction Control Block itself was an imposing structure. In the delivered system it occupied almost 1K of memory. Much of the bulk was due to the screen representation, but it was a large message no matter how you looked at it. Passing the block between processes was inefficient from the standpoint of processor loading. Each process that dealt with the block used only part of the information found there even though it needed to accept and send the entire block as part of its processing.

Ben felt the disadvantages were outweighed by the benefits. By developing the Transaction Control Block, he had set the boundaries of the information to be passed between processes. He felt he could probably go forward with only the module drawings, annotated for packaging, as a guide.

If you are leading a crunch-mode project, or any project for that matter, it is absolutely essential to do some form of data design before coding starts. The earlier this is done, the better. Not only can a study of the data lead to valuable insights about the structure of the system, but the organization of data is closely tied to the controls that must be included in the system.

As an example, suppose we are designing a system to handle an Automatic Teller Machine (ATM) for a bank, and we want a series of controls to ensure the machine is functioning properly. The machine itself can hold

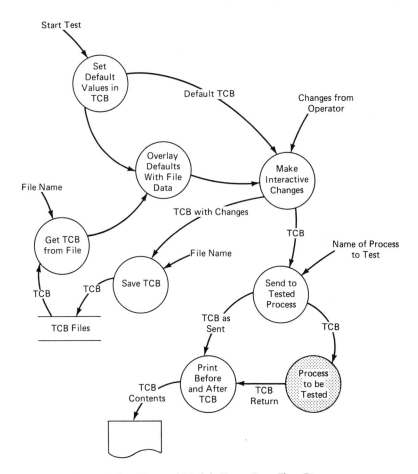

Figure 5-3.   Universal Module Tester Data Flow Diagram.

totals of activity. The program controlling the machine can hold totals of the machine's activity. Is this sufficient? Probably not. If either the ATM or the computer malfunctions, we will need an independent way of computing the machine totals to verify the remaining result. This is usually handled by identifying a specific Automatic Teller Machine in each transaction record. The information required for control will be clearly shown in the three data items:

- The structure of the "totals" message sent from the ATM.
- The presence of an internal table recording ATM activity.
- The identification of the ATM unit in the transaction record.

Figure 5-5 shows how these elements are brought together in the final system. Workable controls are often easier to identify from a study of the data than from a study of the process flow. A common form of control is building totals during processing and checking them later through an independent summation of data records. The method is most often applied to data collection systems but it can be used for many other types of systems as well.

Specification and Design Languages

In going through the detailed design process, the project leader is forced to seek a balance between speed and rigor. It's not a comfortable position. On the one hand, speed is required. While the importance of careful design is recognized, actual implementation must be started if the project is to have any chance of completion by the scheduled date. On the other hand, lack of rigor can hurt the project if too many design items are overlooked. This leads to attempts to fix the design by changing the code. When code is changed to correct design deficiencies, the time required for testing increases. The code changes begin to have "side effects" on the rest of the system.

There are a number of tools available to bring more rigor to the design process. Special purpose specification languages have been available for some time. Problem Statement Language (PSL) along with its Problem Statement Analyzer (PSA) have been available for almost ten years.[4] They have undergone many refinements since they were first announced. Used by a project leader who is thoroughly familiar with them and by a project team familiar with the methodology, they can be a significant help in keeping track of the design details.

I don't feel specification languages should be used as a primary design tool, however. In crunch-mode projects, the ability to quickly communicate design among members of the team is not merely a benefit, but a necessity. Specification languages are artificial languages and most people, programmers included, have trouble comprehending documents of several pages written in artificial languages. It's important for a program specification to be quickly understandable if it's going to be used in crunch mode.

Another form of specification language should be mentioned here. Finite-state diagrams can be used as a specification for a program or a system. These are matrices of states and actions showing how an input detected while the system is in one state will cause an action and then place the system in another state. This sort of specification is becoming common in

Set Default Values for operator and terminal TCB segments

Do Forever

Load TCB values from file?

Yes / No

Yes branch:
Get Filename from operator

Open the File

OK — Error: Display "Did not Open" STOP PROGRAM

Move date to test TCB

Read TCB image from file

OK — Error: Display "Read Error" STOP PROGRAM

Move TCB image to test block

Does operator want to modify date interactively?

Yes / No

Do
  Display Field Name
  Get operator entered value
    Non-Blank: Replace current value with operator entered value
    Blank: Don't change existing value
UNTIL All fields have been processed

Does operator want to save block?

Yes / No

Get Filename from Operator

Create the File

OK — Error: Display "Couldn't Create"

Write TCB to file

OK — Error: Display "Couldn't Save"

Ask if operator wants to continue

Yes / No

Display "Test Complete" STOP PROGRAM

No branch:
Ask if operator wants to continue

Yes / No

Display "Test Complete" STOP PROGRAM

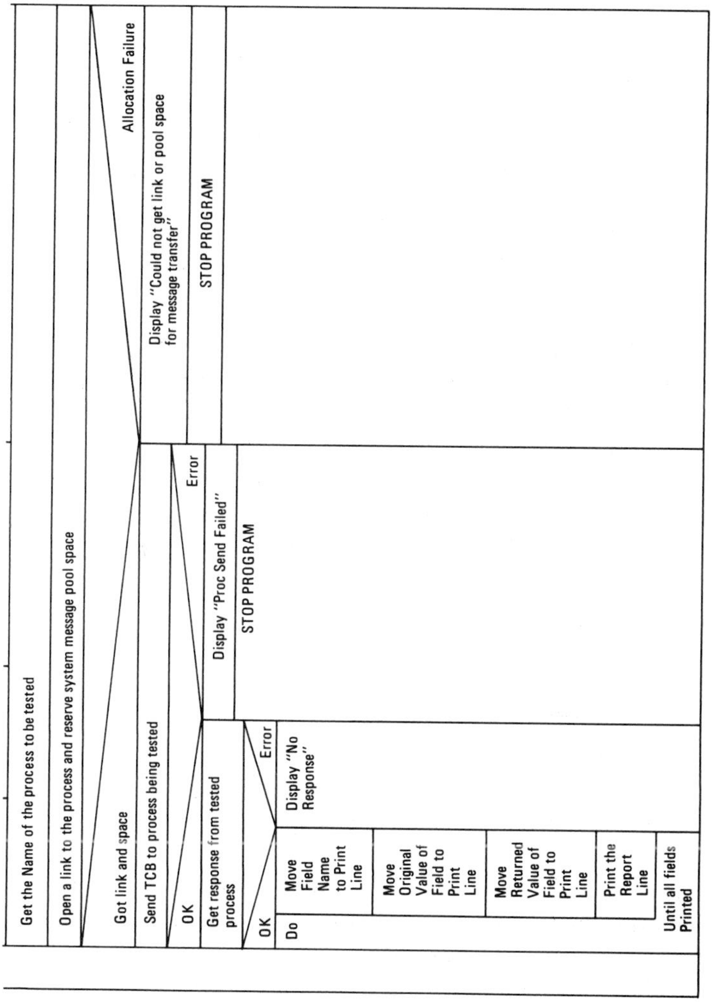

FIGURE 5-4. Universal Module Tester Program Design (A Nassi-Shneiderman Diagram).

79

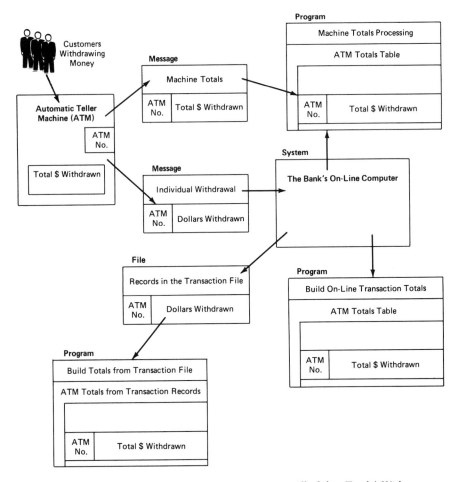

Figure 5-5. Control Planning for an ATM System. All of the "Total $ Withdrawn" must be identical for the system to be "in balance."

data communications work.[5] It can also be quite useful in specifying the system's human interface for those systems that require an operator to deal with sequences of entry and validation screens. The diagrams are sometimes produced by the customer (or by a standards committee) and are simply given to the project leader to implement.

It takes a considerable amount of work to develop a finite-state diagram for a system with more than a small number of states and actions, and you should give careful thought to putting forth that effort in a crunch-mode project. Balanced against the difficulty of creating the diagram is its utility in helping to develop a rigorous test plan for the system as a whole. If you are familiar with finite-state diagrams and have the time to develop them, and if the system being built lends itself to their use, then you should try to develop them. Otherwise, don't.

Recent Developments

Some recent developments deserve consideration by the crunch-mode project leader. The first is the use of fourth-generation languages. The second is the development of the HOS design methodology. The third is the advent of artificial intelligence. Each of these can lead to substantial increases in individual productivity and shorter development times. They represent the leading edge of fundamental changes in the way programming is approached.

Fourth-generation languages are associated with advances in database design and manipulation. Since they are programming languages, they are not suitable for developing presentation materials. What they do allow is a rapid transition from design drawings to running programs. Here are some executable program statements in a fourth-generation language:

```
WRITE CUSTOMER ORDER
PRINT REJECT NOTICE
IF UNITS ON HAND > EMERGENCY RESERVE
        SET ITEM PRICE = CATALOG PRICE
ELSE
        WRITE BACKORDER
```

Top-down system development is a process of decomposition. We go from the highest level ("Manage Inventory") to the lowest ("POSITION FILE [INVENTORY-BACKORDERED-FILE, PART-NUMBER-KEY, PART-NUMBER-VALUE]"). As we go lower, we move from abstraction to detail and the chances for mistakes grow. Fourth-generation languages raise the lowest level to a point where we are still dealing in problem-oriented abstractions, not with details of the programming language and operating system functions. The level of complexity is therefore reduced for the programmer.

Many systems are built to reduce and report collected data. It might be test marketing data, advertising effectiveness data, drug side-effect data, or any of millions of other types of data. A fourth-generation language should be an early choice if you need to do a crunch-mode project with a data intensive system. Fourth-generation languages will allow you to spend considerable time designing the database while at the same time reducing the amount of coding and testing time required. This doesn't mean you can relax; you'll find the extra time available really does get spent on database design.

Spreadsheet programs such as Lotus 1-2-3® from Lotus Development Corp. are sometimes referred to as fourth-generation languages. Whether you agree with this classification or not, there can be little doubt of their effect in the area of data processing. Users with little formal programming training are producing reports and graphic output that would have required the attention of skilled programmers only a few years ago. Some crunch-mode projection and reporting systems that previously required considerable mainframe programming can now be solved more quickly using software packages and a computer that sits on a desktop.

HOS (Higher Order Software) deserves attention in the crunch-mode environment for several reasons.

- It uses a graphic presentation of system design.
- It integrates process and data design.
- It enforces discipline in functional decomposition.
- It can produce code automatically.

HOS, available from Higher Order Software of Cambridge, Mass., is a design methodology with supporting software. The actual design program, called USE.IT, is used to develop a set of diagrams that look similar to the module drawings or structure charts. However, the rules for decomposition within HOS are formal. They describe unambiguously the relationship of modules to one another. Further, the relationships are defined in terms of the data structures used by the modules. The design that emerges is provably correct in a mathematical sense. Changes to the design are reflected automatically in the affected areas of the system and are checked to ensure they do not cause logical inconsistencies. Figure 5-6 gives a trivial example of the use of HOS diagrams.

Finally, the design document can be used as input to a program generator to produce COBOL, FORTRAN or Pascal code. Automation of the coding process represents a tremendous gain in productivity and may, in time, change the nature of the data processing profession.

James Martin, in his book *System Design from Provably Correct Constructs*,[6] gives an example of the gains made possible by program generators. A program was developed for the Buildings Division of the Butler Manufacturing Company. The program effectively designs a building to the customer's order. Factors such as wind load and local code restrictions must be handled by the system. The specification, design, and code were completed in 11 days. The generated code contained about 10,000 FORTRAN statements. *This was a one-person job, performed by someone who had never written a computer program before!*

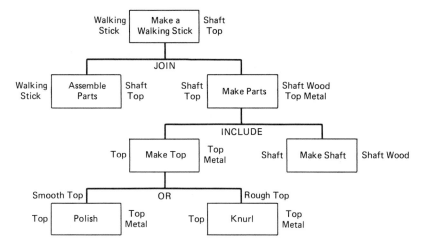

Figure 5-6. A Trivial Example of HOS Design. The important thing to notice in the example is the operators—JOIN, INCLUDE, and OR. These have a precise mathematical meaning and can be thought of as functions, as in $x = f(y)$ where f is a function establishing a relationship between x and y.

The HOS software, called USE.IT, forces the designer to use these functions in designing software. This leads to a design that is provably correct in a mathematical sense. The software also provides automatic code generation.

Artificial intelligence, whether in expert systems or logic programming languages like PROLOG, is still in its formative stages. It appears that artificial intelligence can be very productive in situations where processing of existing stores of data is required. An expert system provides a means for the user to get the information he wants without the need for a program to be written. If these systems become common, the number of crunch-mode projects initiated should diminish. We're liable to learn a lot more about the power and limitations of artificial intelligence as more information comes out of the Japanese "Fifth Generation" effort.

You may feel uncomfortable in choosing a methodology or language you don't know to build a system with rigid time constraints. It might seem there is barely enough time to build the system using techniques you already know. Where are you going to find the time to learn a new way of doing things? It often happens that we don't move forward to new techniques because we want to, but because we are forced to. In a crunch-mode project, you already have the risk of failure staring you in the face. If you have serious doubts about your ability to produce the system on time with methods you've used in the past, how much extra risk are you taking by trying a new methodology that could increase productivity by an order of magnitude?

Productivity is overwhelmingly important in crunch-mode development. All the work we have described in developing specifications that can be quickly understood is an attempt to avoid the unproductive activity of preparing and reading (and often misunderstanding) tomes of textual specifications. We reduce the number of files and data structures to keep the system simple because we know it is easier to achieve high productivity on simple systems. We avoid concentrating on detail because early concern with detail is unproductive.

Many of the techniques we have mentioned earlier in the book are grouped together under the heading of "the structured revolution." These techniques provided a considerable increase in productivity over the "programming is an art, not a science" techniques that preceded them. Data flow diagrams, top-down design, structured programming, walkthroughs, and improved programming languages have raised productivity by up to 50%. Some cases have achieved very high productivity by combining these techniques with extremely talented programmers. Impressive as the gains from the structured revolution are, evidence is accumulating showing skilled programmers using HOS or fourth-generation languages can produce reliable working programs in one-tenth the time required if the program was written in one of the high-level languages in common use.

The success of fourth-generation languages, HOS methodology, and artificial intelligence in the realm of system development will be controlled by the productivity they yield. If they live up to their promise, the craft of programming will be greatly changed from what we know now.

Brave Old World

Despite the advantages of recent developments like those mentioned above, the chances are better than average your system will be developed using a well-known language like COBOL or Pascal. You are likely to be using design techniques that have existed for several years, such as the ones used in developing the Call-a-Bet system. New techniques and languages take time to spread, and existing ways of doing things have surprising tenacity. Do you remember when PL/1 was going to make both FORTRAN and COBOL obsolete? Although newer techniques may give promise of greater productivity, the use of established methods certainly doesn't doom you to failure.

In fact, your task is easier today than it used to be. A number of automated design aids are available to help you with the most difficult technical aspect of the crunch-mode design work. This aspect is managing the increasing amount of detail that accompanies the design as it moves from the top-level generalities to the lower-level specifics.

Keeping track of variables, procedures, and arguments in a design is something that can be done more efficiently and accurately with the aid of a computer than by human effort alone. The widespread acceptance of computer-aided design (CAD) in electrical, mechanical, aeronautical and other areas of engineering should be a clear sign of the potential for similar techniques in software development.

Most designers will agree that the most valuable mechanical aid in the design process is the ubiquitous whiteboard with a set of colored markers. It's easy to use, very flexible, and its size is such that several people can see what's on it at the same time. But once you feel the design on the whiteboard is correct, what's the next step?

You really should consider putting the design into a microcomputer. Several packages are available to support the design process and make your life *much* easier. Design management software that runs on a personal computer system includes *Excelerator*™ from InTech, DFDdraw™ from McDonnell-Douglas, CASE–2000™ from NASTEC, and Analyst Toolkit™ from Yourdon.

Before we look at the Analyst Toolkit,™ it will pay to reconsider what is going on during the crunch-mode development process. As the system is designed and implemented from the top down, coding and testing will be underway on some parts of the system before design has been completed for other parts. As the system grows, errors in the design will come to light. For example, in the Call-a-Bet system it became clear that two different status values were required: one that would be used from the top process level to any other level, and another that allowed specific signalling between two adjacent levels. The Transaction Control Block had to be changed to accommodate the second status value. It took a lot of hand checking to insure the change was made smoothly.

The work involved in designing a system is not the same as the work required to manage change to the design as it exists. The management of design changes is the area where software like Yourdon's Analyst Toolkit™ can provide the greatest benefit to the project leader. As one user of the software told me, "If you use your whiteboard and I use my program to do the original design, it'll take us both about the same amount of time. You might even be faster. But if we have to change the design two days later, I'll beat your time by ten to one."

Productivity gains of an order of magnitude are too important to be ignored on a crunch-mode project. What does the software do that can help to that extent? First, it provides for documentation of the design using a consistent notation. Analyst Toolkit™ stores data flow diagrams as graphic images. These graphic images—besides being neater and more readable than their hand-drawn predecessors—use a common set of symbols and labeling conventions. Anyone who's gone back over design drawings containing personal idiosyncracies can appreciate this benefit.

Second, it allows for changes in the existing drawings without requiring that the whole thing be redone. You can move graphic elements around as if they were paper cut-out figures on a tabletop and the package will redraw the connectors automatically. The amount of time required to change existing design drawings by hand sometimes forces this critical work to be left undone. Rather than redrawing, changes are added to the diagram using colored markers. After three or four changes the drawing may be very colorful but hard to understand.

Third, Analyst Toolkit® checks to see if your data flow diagrams are syntactically correct. We don't always think of data flow diagrams in a rigorous sense and, as a result, we sometimes walk away from the design session clutching diagrams that have three data flows entering a processing node but none coming out. The software will check for problems like these and report them to the user. At the point of entry into the documentation set, the package helps insure the documentation is complete.

Fourth, and by far most important, Analyst Toolkit® links the data flows to a data dictionary. Since it does this, it can trace the impact of changes in the data structures throughout the system. When drawings are changed to show a data item flowing out from a processing node, the software can check to see if it actually entered the node. The software can even set up the initial data dictionary entries from the data flows included in the diagrams.

I've taken the Analyst Toolkit® and gone through the part of the Call-a-Bet system that handles payment of IRS Winnings; these are payoffs for successful long-shot bets. If the odds were greater than 300 to 1 and the payoff was over $600, the IRS must be notified that the payoff occurred. With the same odds, if the payoff was over $1,000, the IRS demands 20% be deducted from the payoff amount. In either case, the person who won the bet must fill out an IRS tax reporting form. All this is normally handled at a special window at the racetrack. With telephone betting, the person who won the bet isn't at the track. A set of drawings and reports, Figures 5-7a through 5-7d, illustrate how design management software can help as the design changes.

We've used Yourdon's Analyst Toolkit® for our example because it shows clearly the sort of benefit an automated design management tool can provide. Excelerator® from Index Technology Corp., CASE-2000® from NASTEC, and DFDraw® from McDonnell-Douglas are similar products, although details vary among them. Both Yourdon and McDonnell-Douglas provide demo systems that let you get a feel for the tools.

```
                                                    PAGE    1

                        USAGE OF DICTIONARY ENTRIES
                             12/12/85 16:36:00

USAGE OF SOC_SEC_NO

 - IN DIAGRAMS
        3.1                        ADD NEW ACCOUNT
        3.2                        DISPLAY ACCOUNT DATA
        3.3                        CHANGE ACCOUNT DATA
        3.4                        IRS WINNINGS PROCESSING
        7.6                        IRS PENDING REPORT
        8.1                        TRANSACTION FILE LIST REPORT

 - IN SPECS
        3.6                        IRS WITHOLDING PROCEDURES

 - IN DICTIONARY
        ACCOUNT_REC
        TAX_NOTICE
        IRS_TRANSACTION_REC
        IRS_TOTALS_MESSAGE
        IRS_RPT_DETAIL_LINE
```

Figure 5-7 (a).   In the original design, the social security number for the account holder was kept in the account record. The customer did not want this done, preferring to have the account holder supply his social security number when the tax form was returned.

As a first step, the data dictionary was checked to see where the social security number was used. The Usage of Dictionary Entries report showed all diagrams and specifications that referenced the social security number.

The development of this design management software is a real help to the crunch-mode project manager, and given the cost of the hardware and software required, it should be affordable (and cost-effective) for any but the smallest projects.

The Choice of a Programming Language

The programming language used will have a considerable effect on the productivity of the project team. From the standpoint of a crunch-mode project leader, available languages generally fall into three categories. The first is assembly language, which should be used only as a very last resort. The second is languages that lack the necessary operators to easily support structured programming. These are languages like FORTRAN, APL, and most versions of BASIC. Something close to structured program-

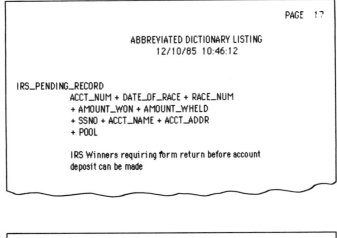

Figure 5-7 (b). A check of the data dictionary, using the abbreviated listing report, showed that the social security number was also carried under another name. Another Usage report (see Figure 5-7a) was run to find out where the data item "SSNO" was used.

ming is possible in these languages, but it is not "natural." Languages in this category should be avoided if better alternatives are available. The third language category is block-structured languages like Pascal, C, PL/1 or any of the ALGOL derivatives. One of these should be your choice if you are forced to use a commonly available language. Block-structured languages have operators that directly support structured programming's iteration and decision forms. They make it easy to read the structure and control flow of the program and thus make it easier to avoid errors in coding. There doesn't appear to be a great deal of difference between the individual block-structured languages as far as productivity is concerned, and programmers who know one of these languages seem to pick up other ones quickly.

It is possible to write structured programs in COBOL, and many books are available to teach the necessary techniques. Well-written COBOL programs are easy to read and maintain, and modern COBOL com-

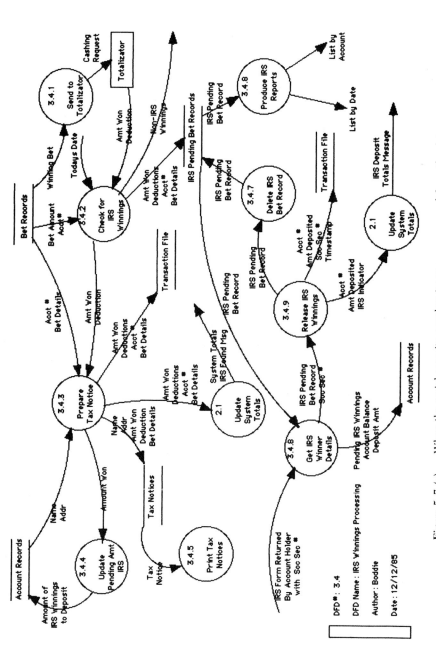

Figure 5-7 (c). When the social security number items were removed from the data flows in the original data flow diagram, the "Redraw" function was used to produce an updated copy. The drawing was then used as input to the data dictionary process, allowing the data dictionary to automatically note the changes.

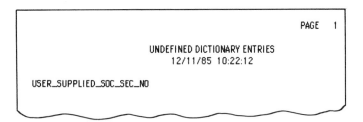

Figure 5-7 (d). After the revised data flow diagram had been submitted, the Undefined Entries report was run as a check to ensure nothing was added to the system without being defined. The item that turned up was subsequently defined by using the data dictionary maintenance functions.

pilers generate efficient code. Unfortunately, many COBOL programs (and COBOL programmers) do not reflect the structured approach. I've found the biggest drawback to COBOL is its treatment of variable data items. Working storage is another form of global memory. The presence of global variables is the data version of programming's GOTO statement. Global variables are easy to use but difficult to protect. Their indiscriminate use can make it difficult to isolate problems turned up in testing.

For specific applications, lesser-known languages may have special features that make them very productive. FORTH, BLISS, MUMPS, and GPSS are examples of languages in this category. If you are charged with developing a process-control application and have the services of a skilled FORTH programmer available, it would be silly to dismiss FORTH from consideration as the language to use.

It's interesting to see Ada becoming available at the same time fourth-generation languages and HOS are beginning to become more widely known. Ada has many features thought out specifically for support of structured programming as we know it. In terms of productivity, it doesn't appear that Ada will offer any gain over other block-structured languages until large libraries of common routines become available. At that point, the programming process will be accelerated through the use of suitable "black box" programs in the system you are developing.

Draw First, Code Later

Making a drawing before starting on the code is an excellent idea, crunch-mode or not. In order to be productive, a programmer needs two things: a clear idea of what his program must do, and a clear plan of how the program will do it. This requires a design. Designing individual programs differs from designing a system not only in scale but in content. The programmer must concern himself with the internal logic of his program.

November 25, 1980

Ben selected Pascal as the programming language for the Call-a-Bet system, even though the available compiler was a pre-release version from the manufacturer. The alternatives were FORTRAN and Assembler. The choice was not very difficult.

As it turned out, Pascal was a good choice for the job. The control structures in Pascal lend themselves to structured programming and the strong typing* of the data elements turned out to be beneficial. Although the strong typing seemed restrictive at first, it prevented sloppiness in the use of data passed between modules. All data external to a module was defined as one or more Pascal records in the data dictionary. The most complex and often-used of these was the Transaction Control Block. Data was explicitly passed between modules. Within the programs, the local data variables were generally counters or flags that were reset to constant values at the start of execution for each transaction they handled.

But before the code could be written, the individual programs had to be designed. Ben had only one rule related to design of individual programs: "You must draw a picture before you write any code." The form of the picture was not mandated. Each programmer could choose the method he or she felt most comfortable with.

It can no longer be treated as a "black box" where the inputs and outputs are known but the internal processing is undefined.

The two most useful drawing techniques for designing individual structured programs in crunch-mode are action diagrams and Nassi-Shneiderman charts. They each force the design to consist of the three basic control structures: sequence, iteration, and selection. Their most important feature, however, is the way they look different than code. The program design remains an abstraction, and the abstraction can be understood far more quickly than the code it represents.

Many programmers use "structured English" or "pseudocode" when designing individual programs. Either can be useful for the individual programmer who has the discipline to use it properly. However each of these techniques has a couple of significant drawbacks that can be especially bothersome during crunch-mode development.

The first is the lack of a graphic element. The importance of a graphic element in communicating the nature of a software design can't be empha-

---

*For those not familiar with Pascal, "strong typing" restricts a variable to a specific range of values and legal operations. If the variable CHIFFRE is defined as being a sixteen-bit integer, the program will only be able to use it as a sixteen-bit integer. It cannot be used as a pair of eight-bit characters without using Pascal's type transfer function to convert the integer value into two eight-bit characters that must, in turn, be stored in a variable whose type is defined as a string of characters.

sized enough. The graphics help the reader grasp the structure of the program quickly, allowing greater concentration on the individual elements of the program design. Lack of a graphic element increases the "time to comprehend."

The second drawback relates to the way structured English and pseudocode look like the final product. When a programmer, particularly one with limited experience, starts with pseudocode or structured English, it quickly degenerates into writing input to the compiler. The programmer doesn't regard pseudocode as an abstraction, but as a first pass at the actual code. In the mind of the programmer, the coding process has begun. For smaller programs, the programmer who treats pseudocode as a first pass at the actual code will often try to write the final product "on the fly." This is not productive. It is not what is needed in a crunch-mode project. When a system is built there are literally millions of design decisions. Most of them are made by individual programmers trying to answer the question, "How am I going to do this?" Without design, many of the decisions will be wrong. It takes time to find and fix wrong coding decisions, and time is in short supply during crunch-mode.

It may be argued Nassi-Shneiderman charts are merely structured English with lines around it. Action diagrams may appear to be no more than pseudocode with vertical lines. This simplification ignores the power of the graphic element in these techniques. The graphic element is the logical framework. The text portion of both action diagrams and Nassi-Shneiderman charts is hung on the framework to show the processing details.

Top-Down and Outside-In

"Packaging" is the act of deciding on a set of functions to be performed by a specific physical program. The final decisions on packaging are made when the individual programs are designed. It is only at this point that the complexity and size of the individual program pieces becomes known.

The usual yardstick in packaging at the program design level is size. It's a good measure. In general, as the size of a program increases, so does its complexity. This is a common assumption when developing software metrics to measure productivity and efficiency. If the design drawing for the program spreads over two sheets of paper, it should probably be broken down. The exceptions are made for programs without clean places to break the logic.

In doing the Call-a-Bet system, Ben didn't have access to any prototyping tools for generating screen displays and reports. Each screen and

January 12, 1981 – January 20, 1981

The bet validation program was written by Virginia. There is a great deal of work involved in validating a group of bets. For each bet, the selected pool must be active for a race, the number of active bets must be calculated, and the combination of horses entered must be legal. The validation process must keep track of more than one horse coupled as a single betting entry and the fact that a minimum number of horses is required for certain pools. The trifecta bet, where you must pick the first, second, and third horses to finish a race, requires ten entries in the race under Kentucky regulations. The number is different in other states.

The design process took three days. Throughout the process, Virginia kept asking questions like, "How are we going to figure the total number of bets?" or "What do we do if a horse is scratched and the pool becomes invalid?" Every time the design started to get into areas of complexity, Ben would say, "Don't worry about it. That'll get handled in the totalizator interface program."

Bet validation turned out to be a clean design. Virginia was able to code it in about two days, and by the beginning of the next week it had been tested thoroughly with the Universal Module Tester. Only one design error turned up, dealing with some unusual trifecta combinations.

"You see, Virginia, I told you not to worry," said Ben. "Bet validation isn't all that bad. What I want you to do next is the totalizator interface. *Now* you can worry."

January 9, 1981

In the Call-a-Bet system, the general screen handling routine took over five pages of code. It was field driven, and the field types and their contents were processed sequentially. Field type processing was broken down into individual procedures, but the programming task was treated as a single unit. The procedures needed to be designed at the time the main program was designed, and they needed to be coded and tested together.

each report required programming effort. Because of this, he was unable to do any "outside-in" work.

"Outside-in" is an approach that gets some trial screens and reports into the hands of the customer and the programmers at an early point in the project. No matter how detailed your specifications are regarding screen layouts and report formats, you should expect some changes when people sit down to actually use them. The use of prototype screens may seem a bit clumsy, but it can turn up problems that can't be found by other means.

January 13, 1981

As originally designed, the screen used by the telephone operator to enter a customer's bet required the operator to press a pool identifier key—W for a bet on a horse to win, T for a trifecta bet, and so forth. A problem showed up when the exacta bet was considered. An exacta is a bet selecting the first and second horses to finish the race in the order they finish. In Kentucky, this bet is called a perfecta. The P was already reserved for the place bet (pick a horse to finish first or second). Another problem came from operators hitting the wrong keys. Pressing the S instead of the W gave a show bet (pick a horse to finish first, second or third) instead of the win bet that was requested. The show bet was incorrect, but it was perfectly legal. It was the sort of error the system couldn't detect.

The solution involved changing the keyboard. A special set of key caps was ordered and installed on the top row of keys for the betting terminals. The keys were colored red so they would stand out. The general screen handling program had to be modified to accept another field type and a procedure to process it was written. The new field type procedure examined the actual key pressed and then translated it for display on the screen and processing by the bet validation process. For example, win, place, and show keycaps replaced the Q, W, and E on the operator's keyboard. When the Q was pressed, the screen handler decoded it and displayed a W. This approach also made it possible to use a single key to select pool identifiers, such as the trifecta box, that needed a two letter display (TX in this case) on the screen.

The screens and reports are not produced only to give the customer something to look at, but also to give programmers working tools to get data in and out of the system. Figures 5-8a and 5-8b show a data entry screen in its prototype and final versions.

If a prototyping tool to generate screens was available, the problems would have come to light much sooner, perhaps in time to affect the screen handler's design. It costs a lot of time to correct code after it has been written and tested. It takes time to become familiar with the existing code. It takes more time to design the change because possible side-effects must be considered. It takes time to retest functions that might be affected. You also need to check the functions that you may feel "couldn't possibly be affected" by the change.

Prototyping tools such as report generators can have additional benefits. On most reports, it doesn't matter exactly what column spacing is used or that the heading is perfectly centered. A report generated quickly using a report generator and data dictionary may be perfectly adequate for not

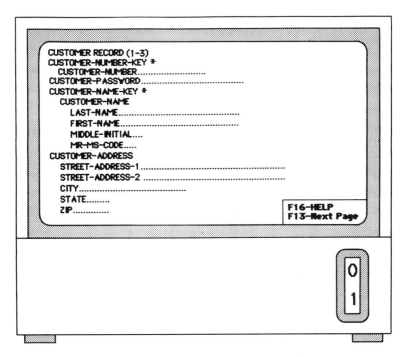

Figure 5-8 (a). A Prototype Entry Screen Prepared Automatically from Data Dictionary Definitions. All fields in the record are presented in the order they appear in the record. The customer and designer can use this screen to identify the data to be entered in the actual application and the order of entry. Programmers can use it to generate test data.

only testing but production. This is particularly true of reports used for control purposes.

Usually there are two types of control reports. The first report contains totals that are compared to other totals. The second type of report gives details of specific subsets of data as an aid in identifying a specific problem. Neither of these reports needs to be beautiful—they just need to be accurate. In addition, control reports should be developed early in the life of the system. This means they may change as the file structures are modified. A report generator linked to a database allows changes to be handled quickly. For interpreted report generators, it isn't even necessary to recompile.

We keep coming back to productivity. Prototyping tools improve productivity. They let programmers generate reports and screens and test data more quickly than they could if a standard programming language was required. If you have access to prototyping tools, use them.

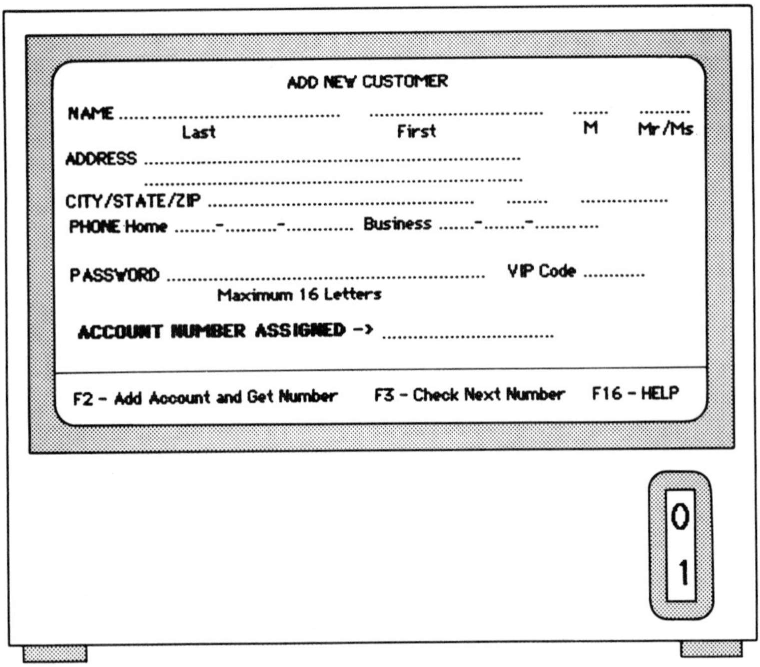

Figure 5-8 (b). The Screen as It Appeared in the Final System. Information extraneous to the Add New Customer function has been removed, and fields are arranged to correspond to the application form. Account number is returned from the system and is displayed in high intensity.

A bank-by-phone service in Florida needed to provide tapes with test data to the banks it served. A series of programs was required to obtain the transaction data from the on-line system and then sort it by bank to produce the tapes. The major difficulty was the fact the on-line system was still in development and couldn't produce the transaction files needed.

The project leader convinced her management to spend $8,000 on a program to generate screens based on file record definitions. Using this program, it was possible to develop full-screen data entry programs for each of the thirty-one different transaction types in less than four days. Combining these programs to produce "on-line transaction files," the project leader was able to deliver a fully functional tape production system and test data for subscriber banks almost three months before the actual data was available from the on-line system.

Depending on the nature of the system and the prototyping tools available, it may be acceptable to do large portions of the system, perhaps even the whole thing, as if it were a prototype. This approach is particularly appealing if the crunch-mode project was undertaken as a stopgap measure to help the enterprise until the "real" system was ready.

Life Without Walkthroughs

In a crunch-mode development project, nobody writes programs in a vacuum. On the other hand, there isn't enough time to put every program through a formal series of reviews and signoffs. A middle ground must be found.

Formal walkthroughs—the presentations of programs or modules by their authors for group review—have become an article of faith for many organizations that embrace structured methods.[7] Properly organized and run, walkthroughs can be valuable tools in finding errors and reducing the cost of long-term maintenance. Unfortunately, they have several drawbacks in the crunch-mode environment.

• Walkthroughs take time. Depending upon the complexity of the code being "walked through" and the skill of the person presenting it, they can take a lot of time. Participants must study someone else's code with a critical eye, reviewing the design and the code and searching for errors or possible improvements. Most of the time is spent wrestling with the code. Human beings don't read code easily. This is true not only of programming code but mathematical proofs and symphonic scores. In a crunch-mode environment, it's very difficult to find time for two or three people to get together to wrestle with someone else's code and discuss it in detail.

• If walkthroughs are rushed, they don't find the important problems. The participants concentrate on problems that are easy to find because they don't have enough time to analyze the code to see if it really meets the requirements. Minor issues are brought up for discussion ("Instead of using the three IF statements here, why don't you replace them with a CASE?"). This is a waste of otherwise productive time.

• The success of a walkthrough depends on a constructive attitude from all the participants. During crunch-mode, programmers are under a lot of pressure. Many times they don't react impartially to suggestions dealing with minor issues.

In crunch-mode, formal walkthroughs are replaced with ad-hoc design reviews. When someone is ready to start writing code, she grabs the project leader or some experienced senior programmer who doesn't look totally overworked, pushes the design drawings in front of the reviewer and explains what she's going to do. This has two benefits. First, someone else looks at the design. The reviewer (and there may be more than one for critical pieces of the code) can grasp the design through the drawings. The reviewer can contribute comments about the important issue of design rather than the secondary issue of the actual code. The second benefit is for the person who will write the program. The need to present the design for review helps to clarify the design in the author's mind.

Because of their "instant" nature, ad-hoc design reviews become commonplace among the development team. They're only slightly more formal than the time-honored tradition of "bouncing an idea off of someone." The design drawings save a lot of time and provide a point of reference. Because ad-hoc reviews are so easy, a programmer may have several of them at different stages of designing a complex program.

There are only two things the project leader should be concerned about related to ad-hoc reviews. The first is to ensure that different people share in the reviewing. The situation where Gloria reviews all Sam's designs and he reviews all of hers is no good even if both of them are excellent programmers. The project leader should participate in as many reviews as possible, and if she writes any code, she should try to let everybody have a chance to review her designs. The second thing is to make sure everyone participates. If you have a programmer who doesn't want to show his designs or produces code wildly different from the designs that were reviewed, get rid of him.

The project leader must make the assumption all of her programmers are capable of generating good code from a reviewed design. Of course this isn't blind faith. The project leader must read all of the produced code before it is put into the system. It's not as bad as it seems. If the project is really large, the project leader might use one other senior person to help, but the number of different reviewers should be kept low. Coding criticism must be consistent to have any effect on programming practice.

What the project leader is looking for is not coding details but for parts of the code that make her feel uncomfortable. These might be places where the control flow is hard to follow or where error conditions aren't explicitly handled. When an uncomfortable piece of code is found, the project leader should sit down with the programmer and go over the design and the piece of code that caused the problem. If the code was added to deal with a design omission, and a high percentage of "uncomfortable code" falls into this category, the project leader must demand the problem be fixed at the design level.

This brings us to coding standards. I use one. It goes like this:

> I must be able to read and understand any code written for the project.

Simple. Although it sounds vague, it is easily enforced. Once I've read a couple of programs written by a team member and have discussed them with her, her code starts looking more like everyone else's. The standard gives me a lot of leeway in accepting different approaches to programming style. As long as it's acceptable I don't complain. The standard, by the way, is not a minimum acceptable standard. There is a certain pleasure to be gained from reading really good code, and when I find some I send it around to team members as an example of what I like.

Where is the Magic?

There isn't any magic in choosing methods for a crunch-mode development effort. If you want a good system, you use tools and techniques that help you produce one. You keep the design out front so people can think about it and how their particular task relates to it. You simplify and try to simplify some more. You use whatever tools you can find that can raise productivity. You make sure people design before they code and make sure the designs are reviewed.

Through it all you look for elegance.

Chapter 6

THE LIGHT BRIGADE

There was, it appeared, a mysterious rite of initiation through which, in one way or another, almost every member of the team passed. The term that the old hands used for this rite—West invented the term, not the practice—was 'signing up.' By signing up for the project you agreed to do whatever was necessary for success. You agreed to forsake, if necessary, family, hobbies, and friends—if you had any of these left (and you might not, if you had signed up too many times before).

Tracy Kidder
The Soul of a New Machine[1]

Nobody comes out of a crunch-mode project unchanged. Months of concentrated mental effort take their toll. There will be times of exhilaration and times of despair, times for laughter and times when angry words come out. The project becomes its own small universe, one in which the sense of time is strangely warped. The pressure is unrelenting. Members of the team carry the knowledge that they must perform to the level of their ability every day for months on end. To do less would let the team down.

The Pressures on individuals

Programmers put pressure on themselves. It comes with the job. There's a lot of ego tied up in the craft of programming. Programmers create programs by force of mental effort. Their ability is tested by an exacting judge—the computer. Writing a good program requires accuracy and attention to detail on the part of the programmer. The task is not easy. When bugs are found, the programmer knows who put them there.

The programmer who writes a program that works well gets the gratification of seeing her creation, the product of her mind and efforts, appreciated by others. A good program may receive compliments from the programmer's peers. The programmer who writes good programs doesn't

The Week of January 12, 1981

If Ben was looking at a program he thought could be completed in three days, he knew how he'd need to approach the programmer who was going to write it. He couldn't say, "This should take you three days to complete." He'd be throwing the task at the programmer. There wouldn't any real commitment on the programmer's part. Ben knew he had to get the programmer to care about the task if there was going to be any chance of getting it done in a hurry.

The approach varied, depending on who was going to do the job. He could tell Virginia, "We really need this by Wednesday." and give her a reason why. Then he'd ask, "Do you think you can get it done by then?" With Lou he'd take a different approach. "Lou, we've got a program here that needs to be written. When I looked at it I thought it would take about three days. Can you take a look at it and tell me if that's unreasonable?"

Ben knew asking the more experienced people for their opinions was not a game. He realized his estimates could have overlooked factors and the original three days might be either too much or too little. Both Lou and Virginia knew they could come back with a different estimate after they'd done the program design.

Ben took a slightly different approach with the more junior members of the team. To Barbara he said, "I want to see if we can get this program written and tested by Wednesday. Let's sit down and take a first cut at the design." Programmers develop confidence in their ability to code long before they develop confidence in their ability to design. It was necessary to lead the junior programmers in to the point where they became confident of their ability to finish the job.

think she's good, she *knows* it. The outward appearance may be self-effacing, but inwardly the programmer basks in the knowledge of her success.

This feeling of success, and the programmer's knowledge that it is within her grasp, is a driving force to professional programmers. The opportunity to create useful things is a lure to us all. Programmers who have moved up to management positions still talk about the fun they had and sometimes find ways to "do a little coding; nothing critical, you understand."

In successful crunch-mode projects there's an attitude about asking for commitment that appears over and over again. It's the approach of the project leader saying, "*I* want *you* to look at this program. Do you think *we* can get it done on time?"

When the individual programmer commits to finish a program by a certain time and date, she is affirming confidence in her ability. She is mak-

---

January 15, 1981

Every time Ben asked someone to write a program, he'd spend some time with her going over the original module drawings. Ben felt it was important for the programmer to know where the program fit into the system as a whole. Knowledge of the program's role in the system would help the programmer design it and would let the programmer see for herself why it was important.

After the explanations, Ben would ask for the commitment. He knew it was necessary for the programmer to say the words directly to him.

---

ing a public statement that she's good enough to do this job on time. Now she must prove it.

Programmers routinely overcommit themselves. The programmer sees herself as the irresistable force, secure in her knowledge of programming. She routinely makes the assumption all will go well in writing and testing her latest program. She allows only the slightest margin for error.

When you think about it, this assumption is very strange. Anyone who has worked on a project knows that many errors that are found and corrected before the system is ready for delivery. Programmers have short memories when it comes to their own mistakes. They simply forget about losing an hour because a pointer wasn't initialized. They overlook the fact that they made "stupid" mistakes by assuming they won't make them again.

With the current level of technology, most programmers will find themselves in a position requiring them to handle masses of detail as they write programs. Human beings aren't very good at this. Even the best programmers make mistakes. The degree of introspection required to really look at our mistakes and recognize them for what they are is considerable. It might be most of us avoid it because it would show us to be not as skilled as we like to think we are.

A side-effect of overcommitment is the tendency of programmers to hide bad news. Again, this is often not intentional. The programmer truly believes her troubles are behind her. She feels she will break through and finish the program very rapidly. Let's be honest. Sometimes the programmer is correct. More often she is not. A programmer who is in danger of missing commitments because of "stupid little mistakes" is a real management problem. The programmer won't ask for help in most cases because she thinks she doesn't need it. By the time the problem comes to light, the only real options are taking the job away from the programmer and giving it to someone else or working with the programmer more closely, giving whatever help and advice is possible and hoping the program can be finished as quickly as possible.

A programmer who is struggling in a crunch-mode project finds incredible pressure from another source. All around her the people she works with are enjoying success as their programs get finished and become part of the working system. The programmer who's having problems is shut off from the satisfaction of contributing. She feels herself becoming an outsider, a failure in the midst of success. Depending upon the individual and the degree of the problem, the solution may be quite drastic.

In a crunch-mode development effort, programmers are concentrating on one small part of the system at a time. They may know how the part fits into the entire system, but their energies will be concentrated only on those things in the system with immediate relevance to the program being worked on. This is a sound approach. Only by reducing the amount of detail a programmer is forced to handle at one time can the number of errors be reduced. In the Call-a-Bet system, the project leader's insistence that every piece of code had to be represented by a drawing before it was coded was a way of reducing detail. The programmer had to break the code down into smaller pieces and had to show the relationship between the pieces. When the code was written, the programmer could focus her mental effort on each of the smaller pieces in turn. This led to a system with very few discovered errors.

But even in dealing with small programs, programmers can run into problems. There will be one or two cases where it seems the code just isn't going to work. This is a dangerous time for programmers who are under deadline pressure. There is a tremendous urge to treat the cases that don't work as exception conditions and add a little code to handle them, but this tactic breeds disasters. The programmer must learn to "walk away" from the problem. She must put distance between herself and the code in order to solve the problem. She needs to look at the original drawings created before she started coding and fix the problem there. If certain conditions truly are exceptions, she must change the design to explicitly handle them in a way that doesn't affect her "main-line" procedure.

In a crunch-mode situation, the programmer who runs up against a problem and decides to work on it for another day before asking for help is hurting the project team. In many, many cases the act of explaining the problem to someone else unlocks the solution. Sometimes the listener will ask the programmer to clarify a point and the question will force the programmer to look at the problem from a new perspective.

Still, many programmers will be reluctant to ask for help. Some of them really think they'll solve the problem if they only give it a little more effort. Others are afraid of appearing foolish. Look at the projects around you. When a programmer has done something she's proud of, she'll drag you over to show it to you. If she's having problems, she keeps to herself. Sharing success is always easier than sharing problems. It's up to the project leader to make the members of the team realize the success of the project is more important than individual accomplishment. Only when this idea takes hold will programmers put their own egos a little to the side and start asking for help when they first realize it's needed.

Project Leaders

In crunch-mode projects, leadership is more critical than management. A project may be well managed with respect to bringing qualified individuals together to form the team and making sure they have the tools they need. A good plan may have been drawn up to show accurately how the project is progressing. But management of this sort, important as it is, won't be successful without leadership on the project.

Sometimes, particularly on small projects like the Call-a-Bet system, management and leadership are found in one person. On other projects there may be a formal difference between project management and technical leadership. In either case, project leadership will reside in an individual or a very small group, each of whom acts as the project leader for his or her part of the system.

> West kept final authority over the circuit designs. But he loosened control over most of the management of their creation. How did the Hardy Boys invent the general plan for the hardware? "Essentially," said Ed Rasala, "some of the guys and I sat down and decided what elements we needed." Over in the Microteam, though never explicitly told to do so, Chuck Holland took on the job of organizing the microcoding job. Holland and Ken Holberger mediated the deals between the Hardy Boys and the Microkids, but in general the veterans let them work things out for themselves.
>
> Tracy Kidder
> *The Soul of a New Machine*[2]

Leadership in the crunch-mode project goes to the person willing and able to make the necessary decisions and take the necessary actions to deliver technical excellence on the project. It involves things like putting up the first design and asking for reaction. It involves spending time looking at an idea that looks crazy to see what the person who proposed it was trying to do. It involves never being too busy to answer a question. It's a combination of attitude and action.

February 2-5, 1981

Alex had joined the Call-a-Bet team when the project was well underway. Ben would later note that he was the most talented of the individuals who worked on the project. At the time Alex joined, the system restart and recovery functions existed on the data flow diagrams and module drawings, but nothing else had been done on them. Ben went through the system design and the current state of the software with Alex and spent some time explaining the working practices used by the team. He then told Alex to look at the restart and recovery functions.

At the end of the second day, Alex came to Ben and told him about a problem he'd discovered. Ben quickly realized the problem was quite serious. It was going to require changes to the way the transaction file was organized and meant as many as thirty programs could be affected. With the design as it was, there was a real possibility a bet could be assigned to the wrong account during system rebuild.

On the third day, Ben and Alex went through some of the implications and possible approaches to a solution. Ben told Alex to look at the alternatives in detail and be ready to present one to the team by the following afternoon. Here was Alex, on his fourth day on the team, leading the group into a substantial system change. The strange thing was, it seemed absolutely natural.

On successful projects everyone gets a chance to show some leadership. As people grow to think of the project as their project, they begin looking to see what needs to be done. Little test tools and utilities get some extra polishing so they can be used on other parts of the job. If someone on the team comes up with an elegant solution to a problem, she may find herself leading the rest of the team in examining its implications.

Since the programmers will be doing the detailed design, each of them will have an opportunity to show leadership in his or her own area. In a group of programmers, the best people will stand out, and other programmers will seek their opinions. The project leader must also recognize the people on the team who can help him find a way through the technical jungle. He must draw them into the design and review processes. He must give them an exposure to the job of project leadership.

But technical excellence is not enough.

The general must be the first in the toils and fatigues of the army. In the heat of the summer he does not spread his parasol nor in the cold of winter don thick clothing. In dangerous places he must dismount and walk. He waits until the army's wells have been dug and only then drinks; until the army's food is cooked before he eats; until the army's fortifications have been completed, to shelter himself.

Sun Tzu
The Art of War
Fourth Century B.C.[3]

There are characteristics of leadership in a crunch-mode software development effort that are the same as those in all other forms of human endeavor. Good leaders serve the people they lead. They provide an example and a helping hand. They take the time to look for ways to make life easier for other people on the team. They don't conceive of barriers between "my" part of the system and "your" part of the system.

Project Managers

Project management is different than project leadership, although the two roles are often combined in one person. Project managers have formal responsibility for the outcome of the project. They must have authority to manage the project as they see fit. This means real authority, not just a title. The project manager is responsible for handling the really messy problems that come up, like removing programmers who aren't producing. The project manager must be able to solve problems quickly, and to do this he needs both support and freedom from higher levels of management.

A crunch-mode project builds momentum as it moves forward. Unlike physical momentum, project momentum can easily be dissipated by seemingly small things. One of the key items breaking momentum is the project manager's inability to fix problems quickly. If the printer breaks on Friday afternoon, the team will expect the project manager to borrow a printer from another system or arrange for repairs Friday night. If the project manager isn't able to convince his management that he should be allowed to move the printer over from the accounting system, or if he isn't allowed to spend the extra money on off-hours service calls, the team will start to wonder about the importance of the project. They'll wonder why they are being asked to put in extra time and effort when the company won't extend itself a little to help them.

Project managers who are accustomed to doing things "by the book" often have problems when they're put in charge of crunch-mode efforts. The crunch-mode project manager must be able to improvise and bend the rules to get his people the resources they need. "Do it now, explain it later" is an approach used by many successful crunch-mode managers.

The best managers think of themselves as playing coaches. They should be
the first on the field in the morning and the last to leave it at night. No job
is too menial for him if it helps one of his players advance toward his objective. How many times has a critical project been held up because there
was no one around who could get someone out of bed, or type up a fresh
draft, or run off some copies on the Xerox?

Robert Townsend
Up the Organization[1]

The bond between project manager and project leader is made up of
shared trust and respect. Each must believe the other is doing the best he or
she can to make the project a success. Each must believe the other is truly
concerned with the programmers doing the work. Each must be ready to
accept criticism and suggestions from the other. The project manager and
project leader must work in tandem, as shown in Figure 6-1.

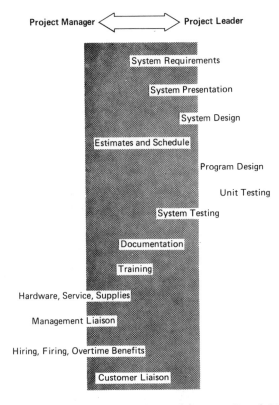

Figure 6-1. Leader and Management Responsibilities in a Crunch-Mode Project.

When the project manager and the project leader are the same person, he must make an effort to ensure that other people on the team feel secure when they offer criticism. Project managers and project leaders need criticism and advice to succeed.

December 9, 1980

When Ben went over the Call-a-Bet system design with members of the project team, he made it a point to tell them, "I'm not a bad designer but I've never had an idea that wasn't improved." It was important to set this tone early. Ben knew his abilities and acknowledged some of his weaknesses. He knew it was important to him to get objective, open opinions on both design and management issues.

He needed the opinions for two reasons. One of them was his certainty the design *could* be improved. The other was to help him better judge the abilities and concerns of the other people on the team.

Assembling the Team

A crunch-mode project team needs quality people to succeed. Programmers who are "good enough" aren't good enough. Mediocre programmers can't give the project the productivity it needs, and they can't assume a leadership role when it's required of them.

If you have been given responsibility for managing a crunch-mode project and find that any programmers assigned to you are nine-to-fivers who haven't shown any spark of creativity on previous projects, get rid of them! Make them the personnel department's problem. Physically get them away from your team.

If you find yourself with some rejects from other projects, take the time to see why they were rejected. In some cases it's just a personality problem. In other cases the programmer irritated her manager by criticism of technical approaches or management practices. If you find someone in this category who seems talented and has some excess energy, my inclination would be to take a chance on her. Of course, if you find someone who has been rejected because she couldn't or wouldn't do the work, you don't want her as part of the team. Make sure she isn't.

A lot of managers agonize over telling programmers they're not wanted on a project team. There's no need to. A weak performer on a crunch-mode team makes life harder for everyone around her. It's a situation that doesn't benefit either the weak individual or the other members of the project team. It sure doesn't make life easier for the project manager. If everything you've found out about a prospective team member indicates she doesn't have the ability and attitude you're looking for, tell her. And don't try to sweeten it up. Tell her the project is going to be very demanding and from what you can find out, you think she'd be over her head.

Crunch-mode projects are not the place to run personal salvage projects. Don't let your project be the one where the non-performer is given "one last chance." On the crunch-mode project team, every member is a key member. You must be able to staff the team with people who have a record of on-the-job performance. They don't have to be nice people. They don't need to be presentable to the customer. But they must produce. Bringing a known non-producer onto the team at the beginning sends a message to other people on the team. It's the message that mediocrity will be tolerated and performance really doesn't count.

Junior programmers are a special case. In most instances they have the energy and will make the commitment to do whatever is necessary for the project. In some instances, the commitment and energy aren't matched by skill. One thing to look for is experience outside of on-the-job programming. The junior programmer who worked in computer operations while he was going to school or the one who helped his church put in a personal computer system will bring a broader perspective to the job than someone who's spent time modifying a payroll system.

Although junior programmers can work out very well, it's a mistake to have too many of them on the team. Even with sharp people, teams with more than twenty percent of their people having less than two years' experience may suffer. They don't suffer because of the quality of the junior people's work, but because of the time required to lead these programmers through the design. You need experienced programmers because they can manage themselves.

If you can assemble a group of good people who are excited about the project and manage it so they can work to the level of their ability, you will have a pleasant surprise. People grow on a good project. Their ability improves and their productivity improves. They will attempt tasks they aren't sure they can handle and produce programs better than anything they thought they could write. This isn't wishful thinking. I've seen it happen over and over again.

The development of individuals on a good team gives project managers and project leaders a wonderful sense of accomplishment. It's the measure good managers in this industry use to judge their success.

Selling the Project

Just assembling a group of good people doesn't make them a team. Each of them must believe in the project and in his or her ability to contribute to it. This belief does not arise spontaneously. The project leader must sell the project to each person on the team.

First, the project leader must sell himself. He must believe the project is important to the business. He must believe it is important to deliver the system quickly. He must believe it is possible to deliver the system on time. He must believe he is capable of leading the project. If he can't believe in himself and in the project, he won't be able to sell it to the team.

If you are chosen to lead a crunch-mode project and you truly believe it can't be done, don't do it. State your reasons and refuse to proceed. Ask for a transfer to another project or another area of the company. Quit if you have to.

It follows that any commander in chief who undertakes to carry out a plan which he considers defective is at fault; he must put forth his reasons, insist on the plan being changed, and finally tender his resignation rather than be the instrument of his army's downfall.

Napoleon
"Military Maxims and Thoughts"

The project leader who cares about his people will not try to sell them a bill of goods about the project. He will be honest about the level of effort it will require and its chances of success. Programmers aren't stupid. The experienced ones will have a keenly developed sense to tell them when they're being "fed a line." Most of them won't be a party to project games because they know they are the ones who will shoulder the burden when the crunch comes.

The project leader shouldn't try to "con" his people, not even a little bit. Little dishonesties poison a project. The project leader must be honest with the members of the team if he wants them to be honest with him. When the project leader tries to get a programmer to commit herself to completing a program in seventy-two hours, he must really believe the programmer has the ability to do it. This is very different from trying to get the shortest possible commitment from a programmer as a means of keeping the pressure high.

There should be no hiding of information on a "need to know" basis. Holding back information is a sign of distrust. The project leader should be prepared to discuss any part of the project with any member of the team who wants to know about it. He should take the time to present the entire project to each person on the team—not only the technical aspects, but also the project background and the need for a crunch schedule. The more an individual team member feels he is trusted by the project leader, the more responsive he will be to guidance when it is needed.

In the process of selling the project to the members of the team, the project leader needs to be consistent. He can't tell different stories to different people. Being honest makes the job easier. Good project leaders also inject a sense of a dramatic undertaking. I remember listening to my project leader when I was a junior programmer:

> What you are going to get out of this project is about three years of experience in one year's time. You are going to work harder than you think possible now. We'll give you whatever help we can, but you're going to do a lot of work on your own. In years to come you're going to think about this system and what you did on it and you're going to feel a satisfaction unlike any you have ever felt.

At the time I thought this was a little overblown, but it turned out he was right. It's a good example of what the project leader must do. He needs to provide more than facts to sell the project. He needs to convey a sense of destiny.

The Shape of the Team

Many project managers make the mistake of trying to set up chief programmer teams. Many companies have positions with titles like "chief programmer" or "lead systems analyst." Who are we trying to fool? There simply aren't very many chief programmers around.

> (The Chief Programmer) personally defines the functional and performance specifications, designs the program, codes it, tests it, and writes its documentation. . . . He needs great talent, ten years experience and considerable systems and application knowledge, whether in applied mathematics, business data handling, or whatever.
>
> F.P. Brooks
> *The Mythical Man-Month*[5]

Trying to set up a chief programmer team when you don't have the services of a genuine chief programmer is a recipe for trouble. What you need to do is look for another structure, one that's suited to the talent you have to work with.

Start at the top. As the project manager, you either need to be the project leader or you need to have someone on the team who is capable of being a project leader. It is the project leader's task to set the pace for the project early on. He needs to put together the initial analysis and design. He needs to lead the other team members into the project. He must have the ability to both understand the project and communicate the understanding to other members of the project team.

You need some experienced people to help the project leader. These people will look at parts of the system and will help the project leader in planning the system architecture. The senior people on the team will work together as equals. They must be made to realize that their suggestions can change the overall structure of the project. In a small group of experienced and talented people, there will be competition to see who can come up with the most elegant solutions to the problems posed by the system.

The project manager needs to find out what the individuals on the team are best at. Then he needs to see that the team is organized to take advantage of the available skills. It often happens that the bulk of the actual coding is handled by the more junior people, some of whom can produce prodigious quantities of really nice code in a short time if they understand what it must do. The senior people help the juniors with design and suggest the test cases necessary to check the program once it's written.

Library programs will often be written by the more senior programmers. Their experience gives them valuable insights into the way library programs are used and the features they must offer to give maximum utility. Senior programmers often know where to find existing library programs that can be used with the new system. This knowledge is very helpful in a crunch-mode situation.

The team may need specialists. Try to find ones who can explain what they're doing and enjoy teaching other programmers new ways to do things. Good specialists will usually accumulate a set of tools and techniques to save them time and effort. You may be able to use or adapt some of these tools and get improved productivity in other parts of the project.

One specialist useful in almost all types of development projects is the technical writer. If you haven't worked with a good technical writer on previous projects (and most project leaders haven't), now is the time to start. A good technical writer will help prepare the necessary user documentation in time for delivery. She can also be a great help during the testing process as she compares how the system actually works to the way she was told it would work.

A chart of the organization among the members of the Call-a-Bet project team is shown in Figure 6-2.

Hired Guns

Sometimes you need to go outside the company to get the skills you need in the group. It's easy to find consultants who will come in to work on

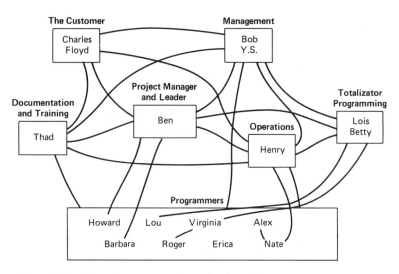

Figure 6-2. The "Organization Chart" for the Call-a-Bet project. The chart
shows "who talked with whom on a regular basis." It also shows the "senior-
junior pairs" who worked together pretty regularly during the development effort. Specific programmers who dealt with the totalizator programmers and operations are also indicated.

the project. It's more difficult to find ones who will make a real contribution.

If you don't have any direct experience with consultants who perform
well in crunch mode, the best way to find good ones is by word of mouth. If
you know you'll need outside help, phone everyone you know who may
have used consultants and try to get some recommendations. Find out if
there are any consulting firms that specialize in your industry or on the
equipment you'll be using. Ask people at the company who sold the computer you're going to use if they can give you any leads. With any luck,
you'll come up with the names of several firms and, more important, the
names of some individuals in those firms.

When you go looking for consultants, you should have specific requirements in mind. You might need a senior person who knows the application area. You might be looking for someone who has used a certain operating system on other projects. You might require a good programmer who
can really crank out Pascal code. Be specific when you ask for people.

If an individual is presented for your consideration, talk to him over
the phone before you bring him in. Explain what the job is and what he'll
be expected to do. Explain the working conditions. If he sounds like he
understands what you need and wants to do the job, get him in and go over
the system presentation the same way you did for the current members of

the team. Consultants aren't much different than anyone else in this business. They want to work on interesting projects. They're happy when they can contribute something important to projects they work on. Look for the consultant to show some excitement and make suggestions about specific areas where he can help.

Make it clear to both the individual and the consulting firm that the individual consultant will report directly to you or to someone you designate. You don't want a representative of the firm coming by for lunch every Wednesday to see how things are going. Make sure the firm and the individual both know you have the power to send him back at any time without advance notice for any reason you might have.

If you bring a consultant on board, you should expect to see him contribute something to the project within a short time after his arrival. If he doesn't, send him home. Lengthy explanations aren't necessary.

If you have consultants on the team, make sure they are brought all the way into the team. They must be expected to contribute and produce like everyone else. Make sure they're involved in the discussions, reviews, and coffee breaks. Find out what they're really good at and take advantage of their strengths.

Good consultants can't be expected to share all the team's emotional involvement in the system. To a certain extent it will never be "their" system. But good consultants take considerable pride in their craft. They can make significant contributions to the project. It's up to the project manager to recognize these contributions and let the consultants know they are appreciated.

Benefits Now

The people who work on a crunch-mode job are going to be asked to put out a lot of time and effort and energy for the sake of the project. They will give up nights and weekends, time they might have spent with family and friends. The reasons motivating people to do this are varied, and often the individuals involved find it difficult to say what they are. But whatever the reason, it's not reasonable to expect people to put out exceptional effort simply because the company wants a project done.

Remember, we're not talking about casual overtime. Expecting someone to put in some night and weekend time for a couple of weeks to get an important proposal or project completed is reasonable, both in programming and in other parts of the business. Putting a person in a position where he will be expected to put in seventy-hour weeks for several months is not the same thing.

Providing some special benefits to the people who work on a crunch-mode job is not a motivation issue, it's an issue of fairness.

There are a number of intangible benefits that come from crunch-mode work.

> They didn't have to name the bigger game. Everyone who had been on the team for a while knew what it was called. It didn't involve stock options. Rasala and Alsing and many of the team had long since decided that they would never see more than token rewards of a material sort. The bigger game was "pinball." West had coined the term; all the old hands used it. "You win one game, you get to play another. You win with this machine, you get to build the next." Pinball was what counted. It was the tacit promise that lay behind signing up, at least for some. . . .
>
> Maybe in the late 1970s designing and debugging a computer was inherently more interesting than most other jobs in industry. But to at least some engineers, at the outset, Eagle appeared to be a fairly uninteresting computer to build. Yet more than two dozen people worked on it overtime, without any real hope of material rewards, for a year and a half, and afterward most of them felt glad. That happened largely because West and the other managers gave them enough freedom to invent, while at the same time guiding them to success.
>
> Tracy Kidder
> *The Soul of a New Machine*[6]

For certain projects the intangible benefits are extremely important and provide sufficient rewards. Working on a project "out on the cutting edge of technology" has an attraction for many very bright people. The opportunity to create something really new and meaningful is a lure few of us can resist.

Good people want to develop their skills, and a crunch-mode project can offer them a great opportunity to do so. In order for the project to be successful, the individuals working on it must be given a great deal of freedom. This gives programmers, even junior programmers, a chance to be part of the design process. It may also expose them to new tools and techniques. If it appears that a new way of building systems will boost productivity, many product managers will try it if they can.

Since the individual programmer will have more responsibility on a crunch-mode job than she might have on a regular project, there will be parts of the system she can truly call hers. The individual pride that comes from taking a program all the way through from design to completion and seeing it work as part of a system is substantial. The opportunity to work this way appeals to many programmers.

The chance to work on a glamorous project has an attraction all its own. Working on software for the space telescope or helping develop the next level of UNIX holds the promise of being part of a great undertaking.

Intangible benefits such as these may be all that's needed to call forth the effort required for crunch-mode development. Some companies have set up development groups where a high level of effort is expected. They have supplied these groups with the latest equipment and made sure group members are attending courses and seminars related to their work whenever they aren't actively working on a project. These companies make substantial investments in providing a stimulating environment in which to work and give group members a substantial voice in the development process. Is it any surprise programmers respond to this approach?

Intangible benefits are important. They supply motivation for the people on the project team. They will be the benefits that stay with the members of the team after the project has been completed. However, in many cases providing tangible benefits is a fair and reasonable thing to do.

The most obvious tangible benefit is money. Money is used as a reward by companies every day. As people become more important in a company, they are paid more money. In many companies, as salespeople make more sales, they are given a larger commission percentage. Union workers get time-and-a-half for overtime. Is it unreasonable to pay some extra money to the programmer who must work nights and weekends to deliver a system quickly?

There are many ways of handling money.

One company pays members of the project team at their computed hourly rate for every hour they work in excess of fifty hours a week.

Another company requires the project manager to submit an estimate of the number of overtime hours a team member will work during a given period. The amount of money agreed on becomes an upper limit, but the programmer is paid for every hour he works. This worked well when the programmer and the project manager had a chance to discuss the estimate before it was submitted.

Yet another company paid project team members at three-fourths of their computed hourly wage for every hour they worked in excess of forty a week. The company agreed to pay each person an amount equal to the total overtime pay received if the system was finished on schedule.

If money is going to be used as a benefit, it should be available at the time the work is performed. In my experience, the promise of bonuses upon successful project completion doesn't work well. Programmers, particularly experienced ones, know projects sometimes fail despite the best efforts of the project team. A crunch-mode project starts out with a risk of failure, even if everything goes well. Proposing completion bonuses may be done with the most honorable of intentions, but somehow it always winds up looking like a game.

For companies that need outstanding performance but don't have money to finance a large overtime effort (such as start-up microcomputer software companies), it's possible to find some money substitutes. Equity participation is a strong motivator. Giving the programmer a development system to keep at the end of the project might be an effective incentive. Sometimes a meaningful profit-sharing arrangement is enough.

Tangible benefits don't need to be the same for everyone on the project. There are always special cases. For the person attending night school who needs time for his studies, the offer of a full semester off at three-quarter pay in lieu of overtime might solve his problem and yours also. Even little things help. The programmer who needs to take at least one night a week off to mow her lawn can be helped by telling her the company will pay to have someone come in and do it. In cases like this the degree of personal attention shown to the individual employee is at least as important as the money involved.

Little benefits should not be ignored as unimportant. The project manager should be sure meal money is available for the people who are working nights and weekends. Don't stint on it—encourage the programmers to relax and get some decent food. You don't want them getting sick on you. And don't force them to run through all the normal expense reporting hoops. Get a secretary to handle the details. Make sure your team members know they can call for hardware service without checking with you first, and don't get upset if you find a couple of calls that weren't really necessary.

Generalities

No two crunch-mode project teams are alike. They acquire an identity through a synthesis of the individuals and the system they are building. Crunch-mode projects change the individuals who work on them, and it's not always reasonable to try to hold a good team together for another project.

Project managers and project leaders get out of teams what they put into them. If they put in honesty, fairness, and concern for the development and accomplishments of the people on the team, they'll find productivity and a willingness to sacrifice.

There's no place for marginal performers on a crunch-mode team.

The project manager must be careful not to dictate the structure of the team. Organization charts should be avoided. Good teams will organize themselves around the project leaders, and team structure may change during the course of a project.

Chapter 7

FLOATING IN THE RAPIDS

You must learn to run your kayak by a sort of ju-jitsu. You must learn to tell what the river will do to you, and given those parameters see how you can live with it. You must absorb its force and convert it to your uses as best you can. Even with the quickness and agility of a kayak, you are not faster than the river, not stronger, and you can beat it only by understanding it.

Strung, Curtis, and Perry[1]
Whitewater

Good projects seem to manage themselves, just as a kayak seems to move effortlessly through the whitewater when seen from a distance. It is only when we come closer that we see the effort and concentration put forth to guide the fragile craft through the treacherous current, avoiding the unseen rocks on every side. Guiding a successful crunch-mode software project is in some ways similar. The effect of the completed system can never convey the effort that went into creating it.

The glamor in software development is in the designing and in the final unveiling. The in-between parts of coding, testing, and fixing mistakes are simply hard work. The support activities of maintaining libraries, backing up the system, and cleaning up the disk to get more space are even less exciting. Most of the time spent in system development is spent toiling in the trenches where the work is.

Overtime

One way to get six months work done in three months is to have everybody work eighty hours a week. To a large extent, this is what happens. Most programmers, if they have committed themselves to finishing a program by Friday morning, will work all Thursday night if they believe the Friday morning delivery is important.

In crunch mode, the members of the team know why delivery of the system is important. They have been told why it's important and they see the resources of the company mobilized to help them deliver the system on time. Overtime is not a surprise to them—they were told when they signed up to expect it. If they can see progress in building the system, they will continue to work days, nights, and weekends to complete it. Vacations during crunch mode are unheard of, and holidays are often ignored.

How many hours do they put in? Seventy and eighty hours for a seven-day week aren't unusual. For short periods it's possible to put in over a hundred hours a week and remain productive. The amount of time and the productivity associated with the time depend on the individual involved and the level of frustration built into the programming environment.

Individuals have different metabolisms. Some are night people, others work better in the early morning. Irrespective of type, nobody's health is going to be ruined by working ten-hour days. Once the project gets rolling, you should expect members of the team to be putting in at least sixty hours a week. If they're not, check first to see if there's something in the way the project is organized that's frustrating them.

The project leader must expect to put in as many hours as possible. This is done for two reasons. First, he must provide an example. You cannot expect people to work overtime if you're not doing it yourself. Overtime must be led. Second, he must be there to answer questions, cut through red tape, and fix problems that come up during odd hours.

November, 1980-February 1981

Since Ben was both the project manager and project leader on the Call-a-Bet development effort, he put in a lot of time. He was conscious about doing this in order to take care of all the little things that needed doing and he was aware of his responsibility to be there to answer questions. He was also conscious of another reason he wanted to be where the action was—he wanted to know everything that was going on.

On some crunch-mode projects, time can be constrained by the availability of a critical resource. This is particularly true if prototype hardware is involved. No matter how well the eventual device is simulated, there comes a time when the real thing must be used. If it's still undergoing changes or it isn't reliable, programmers' schedules need to be adjusted to deal with the situation. In this case, the project leader must expect to encounter "dead time"—periods when the needed hardware simply can't be used. I feel the programmers should get away from the job if they are at a

A Day in the Life

These are Ben's notes for one day of the project, January 23, 1981.

Start—0640

Virginia in—trifecta box problem looks like it may be in the tote. Check with Lois.

Note from Alex—Nate finished two more End of Day reports, Acct Physical Activity and Operator Logon Report. Alex not due in tonight.

Test on check cashing. Format of actual check due in today. Printing looks OK, improve purge message to operator.

WHAT DO WE DO IF CHECK FILE OVERFLOWS?

Barbara in. Check purge prompt. Check file limited to 100 checks. Warning at 80? Do we print check number? Yes!

Lois in—test data problem. Trifecta had an entry. Lois wants horses sorted by runner number. OK unless we need to keep track of entries. NO NEED FOR US TO CALCULATE CHECK PRICE.

Tom—No, we cannot back a check out of cashing file directly and adjust balance. Will need to print check and then do cash deposit.

Check forms arrived—format is off, give to Barbara.

Lou in—overflow problem fixed in system totals. Do we need to use TCB for communication with rebuild? Probably not.

YS just told me I had to train operators. One arrives tomorrow. No way. Ask to get YS and talk to Bob. Also for Bob, when do we get someone to start writing operator manual?

Nate's end of day reports look OK. Talk to him and Alex about rebuild.

Virginia—trifecta prices still off. What's going on here. See Lois.

Virginia and Lois—Lois did not use new file. Re-run test.

Timed new screen clear—response less than 1 sec on error clear, less than 2 on bet submitted. Get screen control back into master and test systems.

Nate's reports into master and test systems.

Dinner—1.5 hrs.

Virginia needs two days in NYC next week. Asked her to get tote interface all the way through.

Erica still having problems with telephone supervisor bet retrieve function. Review design. Need to go backward in file.

Start testing changes in account clerk functions.

Account clerk functions OK. TABS really does print check number on check. New check format looks good.

SUPPOSE WE NEED TO VOID AND RE-PRINT CHECK. DON'T WANT TO DO DUMMY DEPOSIT. TIE-IN WITH SINGLE CHECK DE-LETE?

Look at Lois test races. Need race with insufficient runners.

Can we have a race change from perfecta to quiniela? Is this grounds for refund.

Finish 0120.

point where there really isn't anything they can do. Having a programmer sit around and wait is just not a good idea. She won't be doing anything on her own programs, and she may interfere with other people doing their jobs.

Sometimes it's possible to find some alternative to having the programmer do nothing. Perhaps she could sit in on a design review. The project leader must be careful to see the alternative activity doesn't smell like make-work. He needs to take the activity, no matter how short, and sell it to the programmer just as he sells the other parts of the system.

Some project leaders try to handle dead time by having their people work on more than one program at a time. The idea is to give the programmer some design work to do during those periods when she might otherwise just be waiting. It may work in some cases, but I've always had two problems with it. First, I feel it breaks the concentration of the programmer and leads to a longer time to get the individual programs completed. That's how it appears to me, although I must admit I don't have any empirical data to back up this impression. Second, there isn't any way to be sure the programmer will get to complete both programs. If a programmer is testing program A and takes the little spots of dead time to design program B, the completion of program B is tied to the completion of program A. If I, as the project leader, decide I need program B a little sooner, I must take it away from the programmer who's now designing it and give it to someone else. This does very little for morale, and it gives the impression that the project is disorganized.

If you are on a project that must shuffle schedules to give people a chance to use a critical resource, be sure the person who's supposed to use the resource can get it when she's supposed to. This means the person who used it previously must be finished by the time the next person is ready to start. A friend of mine has been very successful in running projects with these restrictions. He allocates time in five-hour blocks and schedules himself in for an hour at the completion of each of them. During his hour, he runs some elementary checks to insure the hardware is still running well. This, however, is not the main reason he comes in. His presence ensures that his team members won't be at each other's throats because one of them wants "just fifteen more minutes" while the other wants to get started.

The Testing Process and Project Control

Most of the time spent by the project team will be related to testing. Individual programs must be tested, groups of programs operating as a logical unit must be tested, and the system as a whole must be tested. With all this testing to be done, a reasonable person would expect software project managers to put major emphasis on planning and organizing of the testing activities. Most of the time, that's an unreasonable expectation.

There is probably nothing in the software development process receiving more lip service and less commitment than system testing. The reasons for this are many. First, testing is not a "fun" job. Planning test cases, setting up test data, performing the tests and checking the results is hard work. If no problems are found, the programmer receives praise. If there are problems, it's a disappointment to everyone; the programmer who wrote the code, the person doing the testing and the project leader. If a problem turns up in the installed system, the tester will be blamed for not finding it.

Second, the testing job is very demanding if it's done right. Designing test cases takes considerable ingenuity and attention to detail. It's more difficult than programming from an intellectual standpoint. In programming, the programmer has control of her environment. She starts with nothing and builds from there. In testing, the tester is presented with something that may or may not perform in a described manner. By putting in test cases and checking the results, the tester must come to an understanding of what the program really does. This understanding must then be checked against the original program requirements to see if the program is successful.

Third, in many organizations testing has developed the reputation of being a second-rate task. The feeling is that testing is performed by those who aren't good enough to program. This is a self-fulfilling prophecy. If second-rate people are assigned to testing, they will do a second-rate (or possibly third-rate) job. The feeling will spread that "testing doesn't count for much anyway." Since it doesn't count for much, less skilled people will be assigned to it. Programmers and managers will begin to circumvent it. Soon, it will cease to exist as a viable function in its own right.

It doesn't have to be this way.

Providing computer systems for state lotteries is a high-pressure business. The supplier commits to put in a system with many hundreds of terminals into a state in five months or less from the contract date. No two states have the same software requirements. If delivery is late, it may cost the supplier over $200,000 per day in penalties.

Each time American Totalizator installed a lottery system, there was a meeting about a month before the date it was to be activated. The software manager, the engineering manager, the operations manager and the chief executive of the company attended. The chief executive asked the operations manager if the system was ready. If he said "yes," the meeting was effectively over.

The operations manager had responsibility for system testing. His staff would be responsible for proper performance in the field, and he had a vested interest in making sure the system worked correctly.

The method used at American Totalizator worked well for two reasons. First, the operations manager was an intelligent, energetic individual who knew the requirements of the system at least as well as any of the software staff. He was involved in preparing the proposal, meetings with the state lottery boards and preparing the documentation his staff would use.

Second, his management recognized the importance of testing. They made sure the operations manager's opinions carried weight among the other managers on the team. The engineering and software managers knew they had to satisfy the operations manager to do their jobs. At American Totalizator, the adversarial nature of the relationship between the testing and programming groups never got out of hand because the operations manager was impartial in his judgments and because he was unquestionably competent.

In most companies, the "quality assurance" or "systems audit" groups have little or no vested interest in the long-term success of the project they are testing. They have no opportunity to develop expertise in the area where the system will be used. They are not brought into the project as an integral part of the design process. They are the neglected stepchildren of the project.

Conditions such as those at American Totalizator are not widespread. In most crunch-mode projects, the responsibility for meaningful testing falls on the group developing the software. There is only one way to effectively organize a development group to handle the testing—the project leader must have direct responsibility for it.

Controlling Unit Testing

Unit testing is done by the programmer as she develops her program. This type of testing is good for finding minor procedural errors—like uninitialized pointer variables—that account for most of a programmer's mistakes.

Unit testing has become much easier in recent years with the development of powerful symbolic debuggers. The programmer can use these debuggers to simulate error conditions occurring within the program. For example, a program that makes a file system call to read a record from a disk file will have logic to deal with reported disk failures. Using the debugger, these failures can be simulated and the error-handling logic can be exercised.

Unit testing usually requires a "test bed." This is a program or series of programs that invokes the program to be executed, possibly passing arguments to it or putting needed records in files as well. The test bed also reports the outputs of the program being tested.

December 27, 1980

The Call-a-Bet system provided excellent tools for unit testing. Because the majority of the processes communicated using the Transaction Control Block, it was possible to build a "Universal Module Tester" that could be used by programmers developing almost any process in the system.

The Universal Module Tester allowed the programmer to set up a Transaction Control Block, either interactively or by reading it from a file, and send it to the process being tested. The process being tested would examine the contents of the block, perform any processing necessary, and return the block to the Universal Module Tester, where it would be displayed or printed out.

Processes at lower levels of the system could be simulated by a modified version of the Universal Module Tester. It would receive a copy of the Transaction Control Block from the process being tested, set some variables (again, this could be done interactively) and return the block to the process being tested.

The savings in time to be gained from having a common set of unit test modules can be enormous. When programmers must write their own test programs, the results are often "quick and dirty." In some cases they are "dirty" enough to require the programmer to spend more time on debugging the test program than on the program to be tested.

If it's possible, the project leader should find a sharp junior programmer and give him the job of developing and maintaining test tools. This is hardly a luxury. In crunch mode, a programmer can be delayed and lose the thread of her concentration if she must take an extended break from the program she is working on to modify some test software to meet her needs. The test developer may be able to develop sophisticated tools so they can be ready at the time the programmer needs them. If the project is large enough, there may be a requirement for two or three people to develop special test programs and data.

Test beds and stub programs must be designed with the same care and attention to detail as the deliverable software. A poorly designed set of test software may give misleading problem indications or it may be so difficult to use that it discourages the number of test runs required for confidence in the program. If a test program is being developed for a specific piece of the system, the programmer who will use it in testing must review its design. All developed test programs must be kept in a common library, available for all programmers and test program developers. If there are general test programs, like the Universal Module Tester, a senior programmer or the project leader must be involved in the programs' development. Their experience will help define the level of generality needed.

Using the test tools is another topic, and the project leader must actively involve himself in this area. The time to talk about unit testing is during the design period. One question to be asked of any program design is, "How will we go about testing it?" The programmer must be conscious of the need for a testable design.[2]

The project leader must suggest some tests to be performed and encourage the programmer to think of others. Tests using illegal and boundary values are often valuable in uncovering errors. The project leader should also spend some time with the programmer as unit testing is underway. Ask about the kinds of errors she's found. Make it clear that you expect her to keep track of her errors and learn something from them. It's important to encourage programmers to get as much information as they can from an error occurrence. The programmer must understand the error before it can be corrected. The alternative is three or four attempts to fix a problem, each attempt requiring compilation, relinking with other compiled code, test setup, and execution. On a crunch-mode project, there simply isn't extra time to waste like this.

The project leader should make it a habit to occasionally check the spooler to see who's been doing compiles. If there are a number of compilations in a short period of time for a particular program, this should alert the project leader to a possible problem. He should approach the programmer, mention that he's concerned, and find out what the problem is. As a project leader, his approach should be one of concern, and it should convey a desire to help the programmer complete the job successfully.

In addition to specialized test procedures, the individual programmer should have a "private copy" of the system. This will be a complete, running system, although many of its pieces will be stubs. The programmer will be developing a program to replace one of the stubs. She needs to put the program in place and see if it behaves properly in the environment where it will really run.

Ensuring that "private copies" are available to the individual programmers is the job of the project leader. Since he is in charge of the testing, he will determine when new modules can enter the system, and he will be responsible for ensuring that test data files are in the correct format and contain reasonable test data. One way of handling distribution problems with private copies is to provide a mechanism where the "latest known good system" is updated every five to ten days. If this system is set up to let the programmer control the identification of directories, files, and peripherals she will be using through a series of assignment directives or a private configuration file, the programmer will be able to obtain a copy of the current system on demand without disturbing other programmers.

When the programmer is checking out her program using a private copy of the system, she should look for any differences between the way it operates in the system and the way it operated with the unit test programs. Once the differences are identified, the programmer should try to reproduce them using her test programs rather than the private copy of the system. If the programmer concludes the problem is in the "known good system" rather than in her program, she should let the project leader know about it immediately.

System Testing as the Project Control Function

Progress in developing a system can be directly measured by examining the state of system testing. In a top-down development effort, there should be a "known good system" at all times. This system may do very little in the early stages of a project, but its behavior will be known. The process of system testing is one of expanding the system's functions while continuing to maintain a "known good system."

The milestones in the project schedule are statements about the expected functions of the "known good system." When we set a milestone as "Account Entry, Change, and Delete working" and give it a date, we are saying we expect the system to reliably provide the functions of entering, changing, and deleting accounts by that date. If a "known good system" including these functions is available for further development on or before the date estimated, the project has "met the milestone." If the standard system available to programmers who need a private copy does not include the functions on the date specified, the milestone has been missed.

Many otherwise good projects run into trouble applying this standard to milestones. Often a milestone will be claimed as met if the programs required show successful results in unit testing. This is really dangerous. If you are a project leader or a project manager and get into the habit of "fudging milestones," you are not merely postponing a problem, you are making it much worse. It is much easier to handle bad news early in a project than later on. If you can let your management and your customer know early about missed milestones and a lower probability of completion on schedule, they can sometimes arrange for a change in scope or a change in schedule. If they don't get this news until late in the project, these options may no longer be available.

System testing should be directed by the project leader. Virtually all of his hands-on contact with the system should come through system testing. This makes good sense for several reasons:

• The project leader has more understanding of the way the system should function *as a system*. This allows him to look at the final product as more than a collection of individual pieces. Even at the system testing stage of the project, design flaws and omissions can suddenly be found. Only someone with an understanding of the system as a whole will be able to recognize and evaluate such errors.

• The project leader will understand the design of the programs being added to the system, but he will not be the author. This detachment is important for proper testing. It is notoriously difficult for a programmer to really test her own work well. This was the reason the project leader helped suggest cases for unit testing. When the project leader gets the program into system test, he may come up with conditions dismissed by the programmer as "impossible" through actions that seem to him quite natural.

• By putting the completed programs into the system and testing them, the project leader will get a more accurate appraisal of the abilities of project team members than he could get through other means. He is being given programs represented by the programmer as tested and complete.

• More than anyone else, the project leader really needs to know the state of the system. This knowledge is critical in controlling the project. By seeing programs submitted for system testing and watching them work, the project leader can quickly see trouble when it arises and take steps to alleviate it.

• Since the project leader comes in close contact with the programmer's work during the design stage and later at the testing stage, relationships with individual members of the team are kept free of issues related to personality. The project leader who criticizes or praises a programmer has the programmer's work directly in front of him. Both of them can look at the program and see what it does. If criticism is called for, it is directed to the way the program acts during testing. The programmer has little choice but to see this criticism as based on fact.

Direct involvement in the system testing function often leads the project leader to take on an additional support function—the function normally performed by the project librarian.

The project librarian's work—maintaining the "known good system," keeping track of programs scheduled for integration into the system, and controlling changes to the data dictionary and program libraries—is essential for the success of the project. In his description of chief programmer teams, Harlan Mills, who is generally credited with introducing the "chief programmer team" concept, identifies the project librarian as one of the three required people on the team.[3] The often-cited New York Times project was done with three people, and one of these was the librarian.[4]

However, on most projects the librarian's job gets treated as a form of menial labor that must be rotated among the staff because nobody would stand for it as a permanent assignment. This is unfortunate. The librarian can save a great deal of time for a project by knowing where copies of previous versions of software are kept and being sure nothing is changed in the system without at least two pairs of eyes looking at it first.

Most systems have software available to automate a good deal of the library function. This is a great help to the project leader, who already has much to do. By properly limiting access to the library software, the project leader can make it easy for members of the team to get copies of programs for their own use. At the same time, the access limitations make the programmers inform the project leader when revised or new programs are put into the "known good system."

The project leader can also treat the system testing activity as part of the ongoing design of the system. Remember, in a top-down development effort, system testing will start very early, possibly with a system containing nothing but stubs representing many of the upper-level modules. As the first programs and program interfaces start coming into the system, the project leader must look at them as a way of validating the original design.

December, 1980-February, 1981

On the Call-a-Bet project, Ben did the jobs of project manager, project leader and project librarian. The project librarian job turned out to be a happy accident. Ben started doing it simply because he knew it needed doing. After a few weeks he recognized its potential for project control and began to look at it in a new light. It gave him absolute control over the code entering the system. There would be no way for programmers to slip "midnight updates" into the Call-a-Bet library.

As project manager, Ben submitted a report to the Dynatote management each week. It covered the "three Ps" of problems, progress, and plans. Ben found the combination of testing and librarian work made it possible for him to produce the report in less than twenty minutes. Further, he could do it without bothering all the people on the team to find out what they were doing and what their plans were for the next week. He made it a habit to post the weekly report on the door to the computer room as well as sending it to his management.

If there are problems, he should use the system test to find out what they are. Problems in things like data-passing mechanisms are quite important and they can force far-reaching design changes. By direct involvement in the testing, the project leader will develop an understanding of both the problem and its possible solutions.

One task the project leader must face on a regular basis is reporting on the status of the project. If the project leader is directly involved in both system testing and project librarian activity, very little preparation is required. At any time, the project leader will be able to say what the system can do and what's being worked on at the moment. He can also say if the project is on schedule.

Putting the Pieces Together

In putting the crunch-mode system together, it's important to get off to a running start. As quickly as possible after the estimates have been prepared (earlier, if possible), a working system must be set up. This will be the initial "known good system." It should consist of more than a series of programs with nothing but BEGIN and END statements. This is a point where prototyping software really comes in handy.

A reasonable first system will have an operator screen that accepts at least one transaction, a program that either reads or writes a record to a file, and a report showing the result of the transaction. Even a simple transaction like LOGON is acceptable. The user will need to enter an identifier. The ID will be checked against a file, and the file record will be updated if the LOGON occurred successfully. The report will give a list of the users who are logged on and the terminals where they are working.

There you have it—a "known good system." It doesn't do much, but what it does is recognizable as a real part of the system. It gets up and running and allows the team to begin to experience firsthand what working with the computer system will be like.

It's important to see that controls are put into the system as an integral part of the software submittal activity. If a program is added to the system allowing the account manager to immediately clear a check given as a deposit, there must be a report in the system allowing the user to identify the check cleared in this manner and the user ID of the account manager who performed the action. Further, we should be able to see the amount of the check appear as a deposit in the appropriate account record.

A system cannot be a "known good system" unless it contains the means to verify its own correct operation. This means controls cannot be treated as something to be added once the system is working. They must be developed in parallel with the programs performing the basic functions.

December 22, 1980

The milestones in the Call-a-Bet system all required reports to show that the functions required for the milestone worked correctly. Ben was adamant about the need to have milestone events demonstrable to the customer. This didn't mean a demonstration would be held for the customer each time a milestone occurred, but the necessary software for such a demonstration had to be working for the milestone to be met.

In a crunch-mode project, pieces start to enter the system at an increasing rate as the project goes on. Programmers working on their first programs for a new system will take some extra time because they don't really understand the system at first. The little judgments they make as they design and code will take more effort than they will later. As the project goes along, knowledge of the system improves and the techniques for programming will be more familiar. There will be more existing code to draw on as libraries become larger. Productivity will improve as programmers become more practiced with testing and debugging techniques.

The members of the team will see the system coming together and they will see their own efforts becoming part of something that works. There is a kind of snowball effect in a project as the system comes together. The long hours don't seem so long any more.

All this activity is both good news and bad news for the project leader. The good news is that he will be caught up in the general enthusiasm. The bad news is there will be a heavier system testing and project librarian workload. If the load gets to be inhuman—and it might—the project leader must try to get one of the senior people out of programming production and into a position where he can share the system testing load. The project leader must keep the librarian functions himself.

Small Victories and Celebrations

As the system comes together, there will be points where key functions begin to work, milestones are met, or serious problems are solved in an elegant manner. A successful project is made up of a number of small victories. They deserve to be celebrated.

Celebrations focus on success. The project team needs tangible evidence the project is successful. The project leader needs to show success is valued and needs to point to personal and group accomplishments as examples for the rest of the team. This is not a management trick taken from Chapter 4 of "Fifty Ways to Make Your Employees More Productive." It is simply recognition and praise for a job well done.

There are all sorts of celebrations. The project leader may take it upon himself to drag other people on the project over so they can see the new function working. The simple announcement, "Hey! Come over here and see what Barbara just got working, it really looks good" may not seem like much, but Barbara will remember it. Mentioning an individual programmer's accomplishment in the weekly management report is something that's painless to do, but it means a lot.

Bigger victories deserve bigger celebrations. Lunch or dinner at a nice restaurant, preferably one chosen by the programmer responsible for the victory, is always appropriate. One project manager I know sets up a series of orders with a store to supply engraved trophies and plaques for notable achievements. By the end of the project, everyone has at least one or two.

In addition to victory celebrations, the crunch-mode project needs some regular pattern of work-free time. It might be a morning coffee break with pastries from a good bakery. It might be a Friday afternoon "beer bust" such as those put on by some computer manufacturers for their employees.

January, 1981

Several members of the Call-a-Bet team stayed in a hotel within walking distance of the racetrack where the computers were. Dinner became the regular break in the day where people would get a chance to unwind. At a usual dinner, over half the people on the project would show up.

Topics discussed over dinner varied widely. The project was a secondary topic of discussion. If Ben was at dinner, he'd answer any questions about the project, but he seldom got involved in anything sounding like details. He was more interested in the other things being discussed, like why Virginia always travelled with an aardvark doll.

The celebrations are never for the individual. They're for the team. They aren't used as occasions for inspirational pep talks. The fact they exist at all is tacit recognition of the special status of project team. Everyone on the team shares in the hard work, and the celebrations are an attempt to hold the team together as they share in the rewards.

It's important for the team to develop a "group ego." This is the big point of difference between being "assigned to a project" and being "part of a project." Programmers are often quite cynical about loyalty to the companies that employ them, and at the same time they are fiercely loyal to the projects they are working on for the company. During the course of the project, they define their place in the universe as being part of the development team. The reasons aren't particularly surprising.

It's difficult for people outside the development group to really understand what goes on inside it. This hurts the programmer's ability to communicate with the world outside the project. Projects develop their own language: a statement like, "It looks like your program is only setting the process status flags to 'P' in the level-one nodes of the Ordtests array" is simply incomprehensible to anyone not involved with the project.

Because communication is confined to the project, the approval the programmer needs will also come from within the project. It means a great deal to a programmer to have someone who shares the project burden with her say, "That's a really nice piece of work."

The shared burden of work and the shared rewards accompanying it serve to bring the individual members of the group together into a team. This can happen even if relationships are strained on the individual level. In those cases where the individual chemistries don't mix, if there is respect for technical ability between the individuals, the team is unlikely to suffer.

Some project managers feel it's a good idea to give project teams a distinctive name. I've lost count of the number of "Tiger Teams" I've been told about. Special names are fine if the members of the team choose them. If they are bestowed by the project manager or upper management, the effect is sometimes counterproductive. The members of the team get the impression that management is playing games with them at a time when they are concerned with real work.

Similar to bestowing names on teams, the practice of gathering the entire team together to ask for "one last, big push" should be considered carefully before it's done. On well-run projects, it never gets the desired response. In the best case, the exhortations will simply be ignored. The individuals on the team know they are working as hard as they can and know they don't have another ten or fifteen percent to give. In the worst case, the request for additional effort is taken as an insult.

I've only experienced one situation where a last-minute push was effective. The president of the company came down to the project area and spoke with individual programmers. He told them he knew of their efforts and told them about the importance of the project to the company. He asked if there was anything the company could do to help them and asked them if there was anything they could do in addition to what they were already doing. There wasn't very much extra to give, but it was given.

Running Interference

The project manager works in an unending stream of interruptions. Of these, the ones coming from outside the team are the most bothersome. If the project manager allows these interruptions to pass through to the level of the people doing the work, the rhythm of development will be broken.

Particularly difficult to handle are requests for information and demonstrations by management and the customer. These people cannot be frozen out. They have a right to know what's going on. The project manager must handle their requests directly so members of the team are not disturbed.

The project manager must put himself in a position where he gives direct help to the testing process. Only by doing this can he get a feel for the system and its operating behavior. He must be capable of performing the milestone demonstrations without assistance. He must be able to answer questions without needing to ask individual team members.

Many managements, left to their own worst instincts, will constantly want to intervene in a project to ensure it's going well. Special meetings will be scheduled, outside "experts" will be called in, new features will be requested, and demonstrations for prospective customers will be arranged. The project manager must be very firm in making the point there is no such thing as a free lunch. All these things take time, and time is the one inflexible factor in a crunch-mode effort.

> A friend of mine, Tony Brookfield, was managing the development effort for a system designated as the company's flagship system for the next five years. The system was to be ready for announcement and demonstration at the SICOB show in Paris. The components were to be shipped over to France on August 28th.
>
> On August 2nd, the vice-president of marketing called a meeting at corporate headquarters to review the project. The meeting was held August 4th.
>
> "Tony, is the system going to be ready for SICOB?"
>
> "I think it will. There's a lot of work to do yet on the programs, but the hardware looks solid. We're supposed to get a backup system next week and this will give us spares if we need them."
>
> "Good. Then we'll be ready to ship on the twenty-eighth."
>
> "No, sir."
>
> "What do you mean, no! You just told me things were in good shape."
>
> "We'll ship the twenty-ninth. This meeting has cost us a day and there's no time to make it up."

There are probably more diplomatic ways of handling situations like this, but the point must nevertheless be clearly made. Management and the customer can make any changes they want to in the system. They can do anything they want to as far as scheduling meetings and demonstrations. What they cannot do is engage in these actions without affecting the schedule.

January 26-29, 1981

One of the owners of Louisville Downs had close ties to a management consulting firm. At one point during the programming effort, a couple of members from the firm were sent in to see how the project was going.

The bet entry pro ess was working by that time. There would be a strict order to the way bet information was entered. A script had been written for telephone operators to follow. The customer had to tell the operator the race he was betting on and for each bet on that race give the bet type, the horses, and the bet amount.

The management consultant felt it would be better to have a more free-form input of data, allowing the customer to give his bets for all races in any order. Ben felt this was not the right approach and gave his reasons. There was a good deal of friction. Finally the consultant said he didn't think the system would be acceptable to the customer without the free-form entry he advocated. Ben asked for some time to think.

He discussed the problem with the programmer who had put together the bet entry program. They came to the conclusion that very little could be saved it they had to go to the new approach.

Ben went back to the consultant and told him the new approach could be done, but it would delay system installation by three weeks. He suggested the two of them set up a phone call to the customer to see if he would agree to the delay. The change was not made.

The project manager must realize suggestions for changes are not attacks on her professional abilities. It's not necessary to get antagonistic unless the change suggested would reduce the quality of the delivered system. It's the job of the project manager to put a price on the suggested changes and find out if the customer is willing to pay the price. Customers who need a system by a given date are usually reluctant to do anything that reduces the chance of an on-time delivery.

System Debugging

The best way to handle bugs when working at the level of system testing is to take all possible steps to eliminate them in the first place. The emphasis on design and design reviews for individual pieces of the system is an attempt to prevent bugs. The project leader discusses unit testing with the programmer for the same reason.

It's a very good idea for the project leader to post a bug listing or find some alternative way of telling the programmers what sort of bugs are being found. This has the effect of getting the programmers to look at their code with the idea that there may be errors in it. After being told about problems with incomplete CASE statements, nobody on the team will want to turn over his program with an incomplete CASE statement in it.

Bugs are not any harder to fix in the whole system environment than on the program environment (unless the system has pathological connections), but they are much harder to find. If a program cannot read an account record because it is locked by the file system, it will be necessary to find which program locked it and then didn't release it. It may be necessary to look at six or seven programs before the culprit is found.

What do you do when you find it? The programmer who wrote the program may be in the middle of another one now. Do you, as the project leader, interrupt him and tell him to fix the problem in the old program? Do you give the program with the error to another programmer? Do you fix it yourself?

January, 1981

Ben fixed the problems he found by himself. Later he would admit if he had to do it over, he'd do it differently. He rationalized his action on the Call-a-Bet project by noting there weren't too many bugs in the first place and also by noting that his programming strength was as a debugger.

On his next project, he made up his mind to stop once he identified the cause of the problem. He could still do this faster than other people on the team because he knew the whole system better. Once he identified the problem, it would be turned over to another programmer to be fixed. If the original programmer was free, she could do the whole job. If she wasn't, she would still be required to review the design for the fix.

The project leader should keep close track of encountered bugs, what they are, and where they come from. If there are too many of them, or a disproportionate number of them come from programs developed by one member of the team, action is necessary.

Unless the bugs can be accounted for by fatigue or illness, the individual who allows them to be passed through to system testing needs to be told in no uncertain terms to get his act together. The project leader must pay particular attention to the way the programmer handles design for his programs and the way he generates code from the design. This is the place to concentrate; not on the way he does unit testing.

If a large number of problems are coming up and they're coming from everybody, then the project leader must look to himself as the cause. He may not have explained the nature of the system clearly enough. He may not have emphasized the work required in program design. The test data available to the programmers may be wrong. He may not have involved himself in design reviews to the extent necessary. There are many possible causes and the project leader must take the lead in discussing them as his problem, not the team's.

A Parting Shot

I've always felt that directing a symphony orchestra must be the most satisfying job in the world. Imagine starting with a design by a genius like Mozart and bringing together the abilities of sixty or more highly intelligent and talented individuals to create music of great beauty, and knowing part of that beauty was fashioned by your hand, by your ideas of what the music should be.

I'll never be able to direct an orchestra, but in a way directing system test on a project gives me some idea of what it might feel like. I get to sit there, at the center of the project's universe, and watch it all come together. I get to see my people improve and I can share in their successes. I can guide the tempo and call for emphasis on certain parts. And if I'm good enough, I can bring the project in on time. It's a great feeling.

Chapter 8

DEALING
WITH
DISASTER

If it can go wrong, it will.

Attributed to Edsel Murphy

Projects are seldom a triumphant progression from initial concept to delivered system. Along the way unforseen events change the pace and course of the project. Programmers make mistakes, design errors are uncovered, and initial assumptions are found to be invalid. All these problems must be solved before the system can be delivered.

On a crunch-mode development, the effect of problems is magnified by the short time frame. Not only must the problems be solved quickly, but the very act of developing a speedy solution raises the possibility that the correction itself will contain errors. The project leader must find the absolutely fastest, carefully thought out and analyzed solution. Such solutions are not commonly encountered.

The project leader must be forthright and open about problems that exist. She must make both the nature and the expected impact of the problems clear to both her management and members of the team. The solution to many problems requires active participation by company management or the customer. The more detail they have about the problems and the more time they have to develop a solution, the better the project's chances of eventual success.

Missed Milestones and Their Consequences

The most common problem is missing a milestone. It's not uncommon to have the first or second milestone date arrive without the necessary software completed. At the time the milestone dates were developed, the project team and the project leader were still learning about the system to be built. The performance level of the project team was not known. The early dates were estimates, pure and simple, and estimates can be wrong.

Later milestones will be adjusted based on the experience with the first few. They can be expected to be closer to the mark, *but only if the reasons for failure in meeting the earlier milestones are understood.* The project leader must become skilled in conducting "instant post-mortems" if she is to have any chance of keeping the project under control. The goal of the "instant post-mortem" is determining the cause of the delay and analyzing the nature of the cause so its effect on the project as a whole can be judged.

The project leader runs the "instant post-mortem." She may ask for opinions from other members of the team, but she should do this on an individual basis. Often the cause for delay is the failure to finish one critical program. Bringing this out in a group setting makes it appear like a "kangaroo court" to the programmer responsible for the piece that's late. An "instant post-mortem" is not designed to assign blame, but to understand the nature of the problem.

Programs are completed later than expected for a number of reasons.

1. A resource required to complete the program was not available when needed. This might be a programmer who wasn't on the team in time. It might be a piece of computer hardware or a software package that wasn't available when the programmer was ready to use it.

   In many cases, lack of resource is a one-time error. It should not appear again on other parts of the project. But in the case where the resource is unlikely to be available during the rest of the project, the degree of delay for the missed milestone must be extrapolated. An example of this type of problem is prototype hardware with an unacceptably high failure rate or a software package that doesn't live up to expectations.

2. There might be a learning curve problem. This sometimes happens with early milestones. Programmers take longer to get used to the new system than the project leader thought they would. If the project leader wants to attribute delay to a learning curve problem, she must be very sure the programmer's current productivity is at the level originally expected. In addition, the project leader must verify that

more than one programmer has found learning the system more difficult than expected if she is to conclude the problems are caused by the learning curve.

Although learning curve problems are by definition one-time problems, they will probably affect later milestones. A system that's difficult to learn will probably be difficult to use. Mistakes will be made requiring files to be re-created and tests to be rerun. These will take time. Projecting additional delays in this circumstance is little more than inspired guesswork.

If the project leader sees that the project will have several learning curves, the delays encountered with the first one should be extrapolated so the total impact of learning curves in the project can be estimated. If it took longer than expected to learn about the operating system calls, it will probably take longer to learn about the communications subsystem as well.

3. The programmer may have estimated incorrectly the amount of time necessary to develop a program. This certainly happens from time to time. If you review the work the programmer did and can't find anything seriously wrong with the design, coding, or unit testing of the program and, further, you know the programmer put in a considerable amount of productive time, then you simply need to conclude the estimate was wrong. The program was harder to write than the programmer expected!

In this case you need to spend some time with the programmer going over the way the estimate was put together and the parts that were incorrectly estimated. The programmer will be making many more estimates before the project is finished. It's worth the project leader's time to work with the programmer so these estimates become successively better.

Improper estimates are something that affects the entire schedule. The project leader now has empirical evidence that the original estimates were optimistic. This is a very serious problem.

4. The programmer may have fouled up. He may have not worked overtime. He may have stumbled on some design problems and tried to fix them in the code. He might simply be a slow coder or a poor one (or both). In this case the problem can be isolated and turned into a one-time problem in one sense, but it can affect the rest of the schedule in another sense.

The ineffective programmer can be given fewer tasks, each with limited technical sophistication. This will allow some degree of benefit from his presence. But it means resources are reduced below the level the project leader expected. It may be necessary to get another person on the team.

5. There may have been a design problem. Once corrected, this is a one-
   time problem, but it will surely awake fears of other design problems
   waiting to be discovered.

   There's no sense trying to extrapolate design problems since
   their impacts may be so different. A serious oversight may make the
   original schedules impossible; a minor one might be corrected in
   thirty minutes.

Concluding that the problem or problems that caused the milestone
to be missed are one-time problems should afford little relief to the the project leader. On a regular project it might be possible to work a little overtime and get the project back on schedule. In crunch mode, overtime is
already being worked. There is unlikely to be any cushion to absorb the
schedule slippage.

Problems endemic to the development effort are much more serious.
If the project leader concludes that the problems causing the milestone to
be missed will cause subsequent milestones to be missed as well, she must

---

December 28, 1980

The first milestone in the Call-a-Bet project was missed by two weeks. The
reason was fairly simple. It took Ben longer than he expected to assemble the
project team. Ben told the vice-president he reported to about the milestone
that had been missed and voiced doubt that the time could be made up.

Ben told the vice-president he didn't want to revise the schedules immediately. He wanted to get to the second milestone to be sure the problems
with missing the first one were strictly one-time problems. Ben figured the
second milestone would be two weeks late if his assumptions were correct.

The second milestone was eleven days late. Some time had been
gained. Ben felt his original analysis was correct: The first milestone was
missed because of one-time factors. He told his management the schedule
would slip by two weeks. There was some difficulty in this. People saw how
the second milestone was completed in less time than Ben thought it would
take and felt the original schedule would hold up if this pace continued.

Ben felt a two- or three-day miss on a milestone was to be expected
given the estimating techniques employed. If this one was met three days
early, the days might be given back on the next milestone when it took three
days more than expected. Ben was being a bit pessimistic about the final
date, but not by much.

Louisville Downs was informed of the problem and the reasons for it.
They were not especially pleased. Nevertheless, they changed the scheduled
debut date for the system. They also decided to send some management consultants to check on the project.

immediately tell her management that the original schedule will not be met. The project leader should extrapolate the difference between realized delivery and estimated delivery and develop a revised schedule showing when the system, as currently specified, can be delivered.

It is not necessary to reach a milestone before performing an "instant post-mortem." The project leader should be able to tell if an upcoming milestone won't be met before the actual event. Many programs must be written and tests must be performed before a milestone is reached. The project leader will be involved in system testing and can see for herself that programs required for the milestone are not being completed in the required time.

Don't Kid Yourself

Project leaders are not immune to optimism. When things go wrong there is an urge, almost overpowering, to believe that problems are under control and future progress will allow the project to get back on schedule. Project leaders have a lot of themselves invested in the project estimates. Many of them will cling to the original estimates even when evidence all around them shows that the project is slipping further and further off schedule.

> If you miss any milestone by a significant amount, the project will not be completed on schedule.

This is the truth and there is no getting around it. What's a significant amount? I think it's about five days on a ninety-day project. It's tough to make up five days, particularly when you won't have the full ninety days to absorb them. A milestone that's missed by five days when you're fifty days into the project is a serious problem indeed.

"Floating" Specifications

What do you do when the project changes under you? Suddenly the customer or your management demands that the system do something you hadn't planned for. How do you keep the project under control in this situation?

Remember, some changes in requirements are to be expected. A new feature might make the system much easier to sell or to use. The change in the requirements may reflect new legal regulations that must be accommodated by the system. There are literally hundreds of good reasons for changing the system requirements. But in every case, changes in the system require changes in the schedule.

Even if the customer believes he is trading off one feature for another of equal complexity, there is a cost in time that must be accounted for. The new feature must be analyzed in light of its possible effect on the processing and the data of the system. The time required for the new feature must be estimated. The new feature may require changes in software already written. The time required to evaluate a series of proposed changes can affect the project schedule, even if none of the changes is eventually made.

The customer who continues to ask for changes must be made to realize that his requests are endangering scheduled delivery of the system. This is a time for diplomacy. The project leader must not try to tell the customer to stop making suggestions. He must explain to the customer the activity required to respond to a request for a functional change. If there are a large number of requests to change the system, the project leader should consider slowing down the project—taking it out of crunch mode. The chances are very good that the system being built will not meet the customer's requirements, which may have changed substantially. It may be considerably cheaper to go back to the beginning and reevaluate the system requirements, as if this were a new project, than to continue modifying the current design.

Sometimes the project leader can take suggestions and put them on an enhancement list. This approach is known as "Of course we both realize the basic system we'll install at first doesn't provide all the really nice features we want to offer." This approach filters the requests for system changes. Only the really necessary changes will be pursued for installation with the initial system. There are also other ways of filtering the requests so only the serious ones impact the development effort.

A project leader who worked on several early installations of automatic teller machines told me how he handled the problem of constant requests for new system functions.

"I was getting a constant stream of requests for new reports and new functions to be performed at the walk-up machines. The DP manager told me I was only seeing part of the pile. It seemed every department manager said he needed a few special reports. One guy wanted to let the customers find out rates on CD's through the terminals.

"I finally told the DP manager I wasn't going to take any more suggestions without complete written requirements, including samples of the reports. This was a dirty thing to do because all these people were going to descend on him to get the specs written. I told the guy I felt bad about it but I didn't have much choice. The bank was committed to getting the machines running on time."

If you're dealing with "floating" specifications, insist the project schedule be changed to give you time to deal with them. If you must change the system to satisfy one of the new requirements, make sure everyone knows its effect on the chances for on-time delivery of the system. Announce a new expected completion date and change your milestone dates. If the customer and your management want to continue to believe the original schedules will still be met, that's their problem. It is your duty to supply estimates you and your development team believe in.

But remember, never say "No" to a request for a change. You, as the project leader or project manager, do not understand as much about the way the system will eventually be used as the customer does. You may know the system well and may be able to estimate the cost of the change, but you can't make the decision of whether the cost is justified. That's a business decision, much like the one that started the system development in the first place.

People Problems

Crunch-mode development is a pressure cooker. People react in different ways to pressure. Many respond well to it, some do not. Some people can be highly productive for a short period when the pressure is on, but lose their edge quickly if the pressure doesn't let up within a couple of months. Programmers and project leaders who have been through pressure before react differently than programmers facing it for the first time. As long as they don't burn out, the experienced team members will act as a stabilizing force on the project.

Pressure leads to people problems. These are the responsibility of the project manager, not the project leader. This is not to say the project leader can't discuss the problems with the project manager and recommend action. Of course she can, and the project manager is well-advised to listen.

A not-uncommon problem is a conflict between two productive team members. If it's not handled quickly and fairly, it can turn into a relationship that diverts energy from the work to be done. If the project leader and the project manager are doing their jobs, the problem will be noticed and solved before it has time to do any real damage.

Most conflicts between productive members of the team are of this "brush fire" variety. They are easily handled by getting the people together, finding out what caused the problem, and making a decision. The actions must be taken in the open, and the project manager must make it clear that her decision on how to resolve the problem is the end of it.

On crunch-mode teams a bond of shared respect develops between the team members. This holds down the number of conflicts. But some-

February 8, 1981

Ben had picked up Nate toward the end of the project and had assigned him to work on some of the "end-of-day" functions for the Call-a-Bet system. He was surprised when Lou came in one day and accused Nate of costing him a day's hard work. It wasn't a good situation. Nate was new to the project and Lou was one of its most productive people. Nevertheless, Ben had confidence in Nate's ability to handle the work he'd been assigned to and he knew Nate's contribution would be needed. Ben took both Lou and Nate down to the conference room and asked what was going on.

Lou had been working on the account balance validation program and Nate had been working on a program that purged closed accounts. It appeared Nate's program had a bug and it deleted many of the accounts Lou had set up. Ben agreed with Lou; the loss of the accounts was not a good thing. But he also told Lou he should have taken the few seconds required to make sure he had a private copy of the account base he was using. He told Lou to load the account file from the backup tape taken two days ago to see what could be recovered.

He then talked with Nate about the way the test data for the Purge Inactive Accounts program was set up. Ben wanted to ensure problems like this didn't come up again. He told Nate not to worry about Lou's feelings, but also told him to apologize to Lou. After all, it was Nate's program that caused the problem for Lou.

Lou came back a few minutes later and told Ben there were only five accounts that weren't on the backup. Ben asked, "Do you want me to put them back in for you?" "Why don't you get Nate to do it?" asked Lou. Ben explained he could do it faster and he didn't want to spend time playing head games. He told Lou that the problem was taken care of and that he wanted Lou to let it drop.

times you can find yourself with two team members whose personalities just don't mesh. The combination of professional respect and personal dislike is not as rare as you might think. Don't play social worker and try to put the team members together hoping they will grow to like each other. Keep them fully loaded with work in different areas of the system. If you're running a crunch-mode project you already have plenty of problems. Why make more?

Non-producers are a different problem. The project manager must first try to keep them off the team in the first place. This doesn't always work. Often you don't find out someone's a non-producer until they've done a couple of programs.

Sometimes it's a question of degree. A programmer might be non-productive if given a complex task but quite acceptable when producing simple report programs. It is not reasonable to expect everyone on the team to

---

February 6, 1981

Ben had a problem with Erica. She should have been producing much more than she did. He eventually assigned her to work on a small part of the system, one where nobody else would depend on her getting a particular program ready on time.

Virginia talked to Ben about Erica, pointedly asking why he kept her on the team. Ben said, "She's making progress on the phone supervisor programs. It's not the progress I'd like, but it's moving forward. There really isn't anyone else who's not fully loaded, and we have to get the phone supervisor stuff done."

Erica finished her work about three weeks later than Ben had estimated it should take her. The programs worked pretty well and Ben figured someone else could handle the little problems remaining in them. At that point he let Erica go.

Ben later admitted he didn't handle the problem with Erica very well. The work she was doing could have been assigned to a good junior programmer without having an impact on the schedule. Keeping Erica on concerned team members like Virginia. They felt they were carrying the load while Erica was just a passenger.

---

be equally talented. You must use the talent you have in a way that gets the greatest production from it. Don't let qualifications sway you. If there's someone on the team who is nominally a senior programmer but whose ability seems to be limited to simple programs, use his ability as you find it—let him work on simple programs.

If you find you have a non-producer and there is any way of replacing him, do it. You don't even need to wait until he is finished with the program he's currently working on. Even if you must choose an unknown quantity to replace him, you are better off making the change. There doesn't need to be any personal vindictiveness in the process of getting rid of someone who isn't performing. Just talk to him and tell him what he already knows. He is not producing at the level you expected. It may be due to the change in working atmosphere; it may be due to problems outside work. Whatever the reason, only one course of action is available. He is off the team.

If there are other areas of the company or the department where he can work, call the managers. Tell them you have someone who is finishing up with his work on the project. If they have questions about performance—and they probably will—all you need to say is that the individual in question had some problems adapting to the way the group worked.

Once you've told the non-producer he's off the team, make sure he's physically moved away from the development group. If he doesn't have any place to move within the company but your personnel department says you can't let him go without going through the "official company procedures," find him a desk in the personnel department.

Burnout

People who have been producing well and then suddenly don't are another type of problem entirely. Burnout is a real problem on crunchmode jobs. The time required for the work takes away many of the opportunities to use the safety valve each of us has. People who work eighty or ninety hours a week simply get tired. There's a reluctance to go back into work each day. From time to time, someone will just say, "Enough!"

It's difficult to detect the point where someone will burn out. Even talking to the people on your team can't give you a reliable guide. I try to wait until a programmer has finished with the job he's working on to ask

---

January 10, 1981

Howard had joined the Call-a-Bet project early and Ben was happy to have him. He was an experienced programmer with a very good knowledge of Pascal. Ben got him started on the screen handler. The design Howard came up with was a good one. There would be a lot of code, but it would be organized in a way that made it easy to understand.

Ben felt Howard could help him run the project as well. Howard had led several projects in the past and Ben thought he was getting a good feeling for this one. He had the right spirit for the job and was putting in a lot of hours on the screen handler. When Ben had to take a couple of days off, he left Howard in charge.

About a week later, Howard asked for a few days off. He had finished just about all of the screen handler and it looked good. Ben felt Howard had earned a few days' rest. He was surprised when Howard called just before he was to return and told Ben he wouldn't be coming back to the project. He said he was worn out and he didn't want to face two more months of pressure. He had some other opportunities that would give him more free time and he was going to take one of them.

Ben understood. He knew it would be a waste of breath to try talking Howard into coming back. Ben told Howard he had done a good job on the screen handler and the project was better for his efforts. He told Howard a place would be open for him on any future project he wanted to join.

Ben told the remaining members of the team what had happened. He didn't dramatize it. He told them not to think less of Howard for his actions; they might find themselves in the same position some day. Then he talked about the real problem of replacing Howard.

how he feels about the project and about his own motivation. I tell him if he feels a need to get away from the system for a little while, now is the time to mention it.

You can't let people take two-week breaks in the middle of the project but you can't keep them chained to their terminals either. It's usually possible to organize a crunch-mode job to have an "official day off" each week. One manager for a small consulting group makes a point of getting short-term memberships for the people on his teams at health clubs near their work, and he encourages the team members to join an aerobics class. He feels physical deterioration has a lot to do with burnout, and he might be right.

If you have someone who is burning out, you must get them away from what they're doing. You need to do this to preserve the individual's health. You can try to keep them associated with the project in ways that don't have the same pressure—for instance, in reviewing requests for system changes and making up lists of future enhancements. Preparing user documentation or operator training material is another area where burned-out team members can use their knowledge of the system but avoid some of the pressure. If you're creative, you can always find something. Don't cut the burned-out person free unless he has somewhere else to go—it's not fair to the person involved, and it's a bad example for those who remain on the team.

What about burnout for the project leader? It happens, but not often. If the project manager feels her project is in control there's always something to keep her going. The time project leaders burn out is between projects. The tiredness that accumulates during development finally catches up. The project leader looks at the system and the way it's used and counts the cost to herself and those close to her. Sometimes she decides not to sign up the next time the trumpets sound.

Strategic Withdrawal

When things go wrong, the probability of on-time delivery drops. If enough things go wrong, or if any one thing goes wrong enough, the project leader must tell her management the system will not be delivered on time. At this time there are three choices of action:

1. The requirements for the system can be reduced. This means less work is required to finish the project.
2. The delivery date can be put back to allow the project to be finished with all the proposed features intact.
3. The project can be canceled.

Invariably, management will see two other choices—

   4. The team must be motivated to keep to the original schedule at all
      costs.
   5. Additional people can be assigned to the project. They can do the
      work that otherwise might not get done.

   It's a mystery to me why these last two approaches keep showing up,
but they do. They are rarely effective. In most cases, a strong presentation
by the project manager will dispose of these two approaches.[1] He will concentrate on the first two alternatives:

   Reducing the scope of the system.   In order for this approach to be
considered, the system must be partitionable. It must be possible to remove
some features without affecting others. The project leader must have estimates for the impact of removing each feature under consideration. In addition, procedures must be developed to compensate for features removed
from the system.
   A decision to reduce the scope of the system almost always leads to a
series of phased enhancements to be developed and installed after deliver-
ing the initial system. Each phase may be as significant an undertaking as
the original project. Because it's difficult to get the people who worked on
the initial effort to sign up again for a follow-on that starts almost immediately, I try to get as much in the first delivery as I can.

   Adjusting the delivery date.   This should be done only after the project team has some empirical data about its own performance on the project. When the date is changed, the corresponding drop-dead date must also
be changed. The drop-dead date is the latest time the customer can be told
the system won't be ready on the scheduled delivery date.
   Avoid small changes unless you are very confident they will be sufficient. If you are changing the date because of expected recurring problems,
push it out to a point where you feel they can all be handled with a little
room to spare.
   The project that slips by ten days and then another two weeks and
then another week and then yet more is a disaster. This usually happens
when system testing is the last task to be done on the project. On crunch-
mode projects, this is not likely to happen because system testing will have
started early.
   If the scheduled delivery date is changed, it must be sold to the development team in much the same way as the first one. In a sense, a slipped
delivery date is a vote of confidence in the project team. Their manage-

ment and the customer are showing their faith the team can complete the project.

A cancellation is another thing. It's a letdown for everyone associated with the project. When the development is stopped, it's difficult to remember there was always a fair chance the project might not succeed. People on the team will feel they have put in tremendous effort only to be stabbed in the back. It's an understandable attitude. In many companies, excellent work done on a project that's not completed never gets noticed.

There is no easy way to tell a project team the system has been cancelled. The project manager might just as well tell it straight to the group as a whole and answer any questions as best she can. I think it's less painful when a crunch-mode job dies than when a normal one expires. Although it takes a lot of energy, the crunch-mode project doesn't take up years of a person's life. Also, when it's killed it is stopped cleanly; it is not allowed to limp along with reductions in resources and money until eventually it disappears.

The only saving grace on a canceled project is the knowledge that one really put out his or her "best effort." As time goes on, most programmers will work on several projects. Some will be canceled and some will be completed. Completions are nice when they happen, but the day-to-day satisfactions in the craft of building systems are what keep many of us in this business. The knowledge that one has worked hard and worked well is not a trivial reward, even if the work itself vanishes.

Chapter 9

ARRIVING ON TIME

It ain't over until it's over.

Casey Stengel

If the project has met its milestones and the system has come together smoothly, there should only be a few thousand little details to attend to in order to finish the job. Most of these details involve fitting the system into the world where it will be used. For months the only people using it have been the people who built it. They might think it's a great system, but at this point it's only their opinion.

On a crunch-mode effort, most of the energy is spent on getting the system to run. There is so much concentration on this problem that the project leader may lose track of the things to be done outside the system. As the development effort draws to a close, this unfinished business will come back to haunt him.

Documentation

A system needs two kinds of documentation—development documentation and user documentation. We've already talked about development documentation. It's made up mostly of drawings used by programmers as they design their programs. It is produced as the system is being developed, *not* after the code has been written.

On some projects there is a rush at the end to produce "program documentation"—descriptions of the code that's in the system. This is done in the name of maintenance. What it is, really, is stupidity. Development documentation is used to help the programmer do the job of developing her programs. That's the only possible use for it. The programmer, as she builds her programs, uses her design documents and puts comments in her code. The comments identify the program and describe its inputs and outputs. Other comments are used to make the code easier for other people to read. These comments are the "program documentation." They are put in the program not out of deference to maintenance, but because the project leader will insist on it as good programming practice.

The design documents should be collected by the project leader and cross-referenced to the program name. If a technical writer is available, he can help develop an index or have some of the less artistic efforts redrawn for legibility. The use of microcomputer-based design management software can be very useful in getting this accomplished. There shouldn't be any time spent on useless exercises like developing three-volume sets of textual program descriptions that will be out-of-date before they are completed.

User documentation is another thing. Good documentation can make a limited system look very good to its users, just as poor documentation can make them detest an otherwise excellent one. Preparing good user documentation is not a trivial job. It requires someone who understands the user, understands the system, understands the way they will work best together and is able to organize all this understanding so it is useful. The job is beyond the ability of most programmers and project leaders.

If you are running a crunch-mode job, get a good technical writer assigned to it as early as possible. Once you get him, don't treat him like a second-class citizen just because he isn't writing code. Good technical writers are skilled professionals and they are every bit as proud of their ability as good programmers are of theirs.

Try to arrange it so the technical writer learns as much about the system as possible. Have him put in some time at the customer's site so he can learn how the system is to be used. Get him involved in testing the system; listen to his suggestions. Crunch-mode projects get caught up in their own little world and the technical writer can help the project by injecting the viewpoint of the system user rather than the system developer.

It's a good idea to have the technical writer's documentation reviewed by the people who built the system. Looking at the system from the outside, it's possible for the writer to become confused about the actual workings of some of the system functions. If his work is reviewed by the people who built the functions, these errors will be caught.

Good user documentation must be usable. It needs to be organized so users can find what they need to know when they need to know it. The best user material I've seen was organized on three levels: operator's "quick reference cards," an operator's guide, and an operator supervisor's guide, which contained all the operator material as well. Each function described in the operator's guide had a green section giving normal operating procedures, a yellow section giving hints and shortcuts, and a red section giving information about errors and how to handle them.

This documentation had no cross-referencing at the function level. Everything you needed to know was right there, even if it contained material repeated in fifty other places. There was a "Getting Started" section that guided the operator through some sample transactions. There were pictures of the screens the operator would see.

March 3, 1981

User documentation on the Call-a-Bet project was not very good. Ben didn't have the time to do it himself, and no one else on the team had time to take care of it. Eventually the marketing manager took it upon himself to develop it. He used the system and came to Ben with questions when it did something he didn't understand.

Ben never saw the material until he went to Louisville for the installation. It was all text material and it contained some minor inaccuracies. Fortunately, the marketing manager was a first-class instructor. The operators seemed to understand the system and they were handling the test exercises well. Ben shuddered to think about how lucky the project was.

When you get your technical writer, provide him with the equipment he needs to do the job. In many cases this means a personal computer system with good graphics support. Be sure to let him know about any changes you make to existing parts of the system; they may require him to change the documentation as well.

Training

User documentation and user training are sometimes grouped in a common mental image. Wrong! Training is not the same as documentation. While the documentation will be used in training, its primary function is for reference after training has been completed. Training materials such as slides, posters, videotapes, sample exercises, and proficiency tests are not the same as user reference manuals.

Training is best handled by specialists. The ability to teach a user does not come naturally, and an inept presentation of the system can spoil an installation. If your company has a training department, ask them to help.

Go outside the company if you must, but get someone who is experienced in teaching groups of people how to use computer systems.

Development of training material takes a lot of time. You should try to give the people responsible for it some access to the system as early in the project as possible. Just like the technical writer producing the documentation, the training people need to get a feel for the system and the way it will be used.

Because development of training materials must take place in a limited time, some of the most effective techniques cannot be used. Interactive simulation of an operator workstation using computer-aided instruction can be very effective for certain systems, but there is seldom time to develop it on a crunch-mode schedule.

Training, like other parts of the system, needs to be tested. The best place to test training is with the marketing staff. They will be familiar with the user and can understand the way the system will be used. The company will often benefit if the marketing staff has hands-on exposure to the system. It will give them a feel for the capabilities of the system they could not get from presentations by the development group.

March 11, 1981

On the Call-a-Bet project, there was a set of special programs to look into files and change file contents if required. Virginia had built a number of them; she called them "torquers." The programs were secured by special password access to prevent their use by the operations staff at the track.

On the second night of operation, a problem was detected. The amount the totalizator indicated as paid out for the daily double did not balance with the sum of the amounts paid in the main totalizator to patrons at the track and the amounts paid to Call-a-Bet customers who phoned in their bets.

Ben and Virginia looked at some bets in the Call-a-Bet system that should have been winners, but they weren't marked as such. They looked for a daily double bet that had been marked as a winner and when they found one they understood the problem. The winning daily double combination was 8 and 3. The number 8 horse won the first race and the number 3 horse won the second. The bets marked as winners were the ones with a combination of 3 and 8.

Using the torquers, Ben and Virginia isolated the incorrect "winners" and the real winners. They noted the accounts affected. Then they went through and adjusted the "amount won today" totals in all the affected accounts and changed the way the bets were marked. After two hours of work, proof totals were taken and the system was in balance. The end-of-day procedures could be run.

Installation

On a crunch-mode project, the development group will almost always be responsible for the first installation. This can be a frantic time. If the project leader has been doing his job, a number of special tools will be available to help during this period.

Unless you plan for something to go wrong, it will take you by surprise during installation. You must have suitable "firefighting tools" available and know how to use them.

It is not necessary for the entire development team to be present at the installation. In fact, by the time installation begins, some of the team will normally have gone on to other projects. The people you want to keep around for the installation are the good firefighters—people who can isolate a problem and fix it fast. These may not be the most senior people on the team, and they may not be the most productive when it comes to writing programs from the ground up. You may have an installation that goes in smoothly and doesn't even need the firefighters, but if you do need them, you will need them a lot.

Preparing for Maintenance

Systems spend most of their life being maintained. Often, considerably more time and money is put into extending and changing a system than into its initial development. If this surprises you, it shouldn't. Systems change the environments in which they are used. They change the way people work, and when that changes, usually the system must change as well.

In most cases, the development team does not stay with the system to maintain it. The reasons are many, the most common being the desire to move on to something new. Some companies recognize this state of affairs and are organizing their software departments along the lines used in other branches of engineering—software research and development is being separated from "production." The production group is given the responsibility for enhancing and modifying the system to meet the detailed needs of its users over the system's useful life.

In order for this arrangement to succeed, the production group must get to know and understand the system. There are two ways to transfer the necessary information. The first is the documentation. The development documentation and the commented code will be the only things the project team has to give them in this area. If these were sufficient for development, they should provide significant help for those who must make later enhancements to the system.

The second way information is transferred is through direct exposure during the system testing effort. A member of the production staff should be available to get hands-on experience with the new system. One way is to assign a programmer from the production group to the development staff with the understanding that he will have the responsibility for bringing the system over to production. Although this sounds straightforward, it has some pitfalls.

If the assigned programmer doesn't have the skill or the attitude necessary to become a fully productive member of the development group, he will be regarded as an irritant. The project leader is fully within her rights to insist that the irritant be removed. This can cause unnecessary friction between the groups.

If the programmer is competent (even if he's excellent), there's a risk he will become familiar with only those parts of the project he worked on directly. Rather than assigning him as a general resource to the project leader, it would be better to assign him to assist the project leader in system testing and the collection and organization of design documentation. This may not give him a deep insight into some of the development methods, but it will provide exposure to all parts of the system.

A member of the production group should be an active participant in the installation of the system. If possible, he should become involved in user training. Many little problems turn up during installation, and knowledge about their nature and the way they are fixed is invaluable to someone who will be responsible for the system in a few short weeks.

The project leader has some additional work to do if the turnover to production is to go smoothly. She must be prepared to give the same presentations to the members of the production group as she did to the members of the development team. She should plan on being available for consultation when the first enhancements are discussed. She should discuss frankly with the production staff areas of the system she feels are weaker than others.

She must also be prepared to let the system go. When the production team gets the system, there are likely to be comments about the way one feature or another could have been improved. Criticisms like this can hurt for a person who has put a lot into the system. But it's not the time to be defensive. The fact that the system is in the world and working is sufficient answer to all criticism. The system doesn't belong to the project leader any more, and if the people who are now responsible for it don't like the way it works, they can change it to fit their own requirements.

The Feedback File

Another thing the project leader must turn over to the production team is information about all the features suggested during development but not implemented. These may be very important to the production group. This is particularly true if the scope of the project was reduced to keep the original delivery date.

Many of the suggested features will have been analyzed, and there will be notes about their impact on the system. These notes will allow the production group to take control of the new system quickly, since they won't need to spend as much time developing strategies for implementing the requested changes.

The project leader should be prepared to spend time with the production group as they review the requests for changes. As responsibility for the system moves to the production group, they will begin to receive requests for system modifications. Some of these will duplicate requests already made to the development team. The project leader can help the production group correlate the new requests with the old and cut down the size of the "wish list" to something manageable.

The Project Post-Mortem

One of the last things to be done before the development team is disbanded is the project "post-mortem." This is an important event, and it doesn't get done enough in most organizations. The post-mortem should be held even if the system was canceled and the development effort cut short. It is not a forum for assigning blame and giving praise, it is an attempt to find out what really happened.

There's not a lot of time for introspection on a crunch-mode project. Everyone who participates in the project will have a slightly different impression of what went on. The project post-mortem is a chance to review the things that went wrong as well as the ones that succeeded. It's an opportunity for everyone on the team to learn something. Programmers on the team may become project leaders on another one, and the information they get from the post-mortem can make them better ones.

The project leader should be prepared review the project from the beginning, giving her recollection of events and their importance to the project. She should ask for participation from the rest of the group. The post-mortem isn't supposed to be a lecture.

The project team will sometimes identify certain events as being pivotal when the project leader thought they were less important. It's always a little frightening when this happens. The project leader will have worked closely with the team for months. She will have talked to each of the team members hundreds of times. And now, at the end of the project, she finds out about an enormous gap in understanding.

The project post-mortem should result in a report distributed to each of the team members and to the people in management the project leader reported to. It should contain a summary of the important points affecting the project and a series of recommendations for future crunch-mode projects.

Reviewing the Troops

As people leave the development team, the project leader owes each of them some time to review the contributions they made. If the project leader is responsible for a formal performance review, it should be done at this time.

Some project leaders like to throw "awards banquets" with awards of dubious distinction for members of the team. Others will have a more formal celebration, asking the team members to bring their wives, husbands or other special people. Crunch mode is hard on those who don't participate directly, and an organization shows both thoughtfulness and sensitivity when it publicly recognizes their contribution.

One thing that must never be overlooked by the project leader is thanking each member of the project team for signing up and putting something of themselves into the project.

March 21, 1981

This was the last day. The installation had gone well and there wasn't any need to keep the development team on-site for emergency support.

Most of the development team had already left for other projects. Only Ben, Virginia, Barbara, and Lois had come to Louisville to support the installation. There hadn't been any big celebrations as people had left the project, just handshakes and well-wishing.

Ben had made up a special file to be included with the system. It was a tongue-in-cheek "political manifesto" that cried "Free the Call-a-Bet Thirteen!" It contained a few sentences about each of the "martyrs" who built the system. It didn't turn out to be as funny as Ben had hoped, but he felt the system should contain a record of the people who worked on it and he left it in.

Much later, it occurred to Ben that Barbara had summed the project up best. "I'm glad I was a part of this and I'm glad it's over."

Appendix

BRIEF
DESCRIPTIONS
OF
DESIGN TOOLS

Data Flow Diagrams

Structure Charts

Nassi-Shneiderman Diagrams

Action Diagrams

Structured English & Pseudocode

Warnier-Orr Diagrams

Data Flow Diagrams

Data flow diagrams are used to show the flow of data through a system, identifying the data items and the processes that use, create, or modify them. The graphic elements are quite simple, and the notation used is easily understood by people without computer expertise.

Data flow diagrams show the files where data will be stored in addition to the processes affecting the data. They can show dependencies, as one process can use data flowing from another process as its input.

Data flow diagrams come in two basic flavors: the form described by DeMarco and the form described by Gane and Sarson. Both are easy to prepare by hand, and both have automated drawing aids available. The Gane and Sarson form has some additional features allowing physical material flow to be represented in addition to information flow.

Data flow diagrams are an excellent choice for use in a crunch-mode project. They provide an overview of the information structure of the system, they can be quickly prepared, and they make an excellent presentation tool for customers.

However, they should not be used alone. Data flow diagrams do not provide a guide to selecting a program architecture. They are not able to show timing dependence for systems that require it, and process interdependence is often not clear. Further, although they show the use of data, they do not deal with the way data is structured in the system.

The standard references for Data flow diagrams are *Structured Analysis and System Specification* by Tom DeMarco, published by Yourdon Press, and *Structured Systems Analysis: Tools and Techniques* by Chris Gane and Trish Sarson, published by IST, Inc. of New York.

Automated design aids are the Analyst Toolkit™ from Yourdon, Inc. of New York, Excelerator™, produced by InTech of Cambridge, Mass., and DFDdraw™ from IST (a division of McDonnell Douglas) of St. Louis, Mo. The latter two use the Gane and Sarson form. Each of these programs can be run on an IBM™ Personal Computer or compatible unit. All require graphics support hardware.

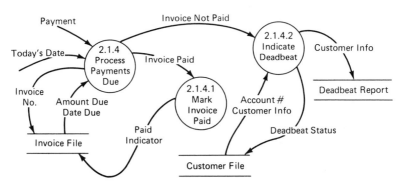

Data Flow Diagram—DeMarco Form.

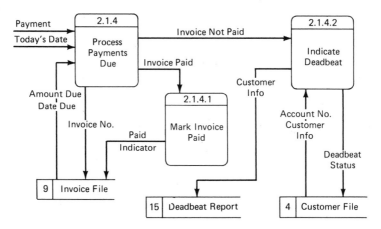

Data Flow Diagram—Gane & Sarson Form.

Structure Charts

Structure charts are composite tools that make it possible to show both processing and data flows in one representation. The use of structure charts is usually presented as a second stage of the system development process, following the creation of a set of data flow diagrams.

Structure charts are best considered as a design tool, not as a technique for presentations to the customer. They follow top-down control rules, and their notation is easy to master although some of the terminology surrounding them may seem unusual. The development of the charts is part of the structured design methodology, which places emphasis on evaluating the coupling and cohesion between modules.

Although data flows are shown passing between modules, the overall structure of the data cannot be determined from the structure charts. One sees only discrete items. If you are planning on using structure charts, you will also need a form of data design documentation to go with them.

Production of structure charts is supported by software from Yourdon, Inc. of New York, InTech of Cambridge, Mass., and McDonnell Douglas Automation Company of St. Louis, Mo.

I have not found structure charts to be useful in crunch-mode projects. The time spent in creating them does not provide significantly better information about data flow and process structuring than is directly available from the data flow diagrams and Warnier-Orr diagrams, both of which take less time to produce. In crunch-mode, there is not enough time

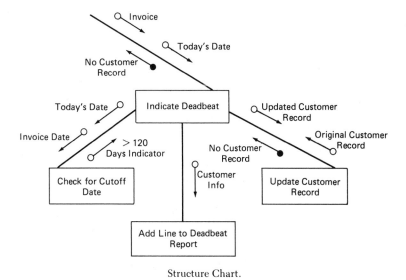

Structure Chart.

to manually maintain the exact data and control flows for each module as the system changes, and this is the area where structured design could give the greatest benefit. The use of automated support tools should overcome this problem.

The standard reference on structure charts is *Structured Design* by Yourdon and Constantine. It is published by Prentice-Hall of Englewood Cliffs, N.J.

Nassi-Shneiderman Charts

Nassi-Shneiderman charts are a classic example of the good news— bad news. The good news is very good. Nassi-Shneiderman charts are excellent tools for detailed program design.

The excellence comes primarily from the graphic organization of the chart. The constructs of structured programming can clearly be seen, and it's very easy to follow program flow from the "top" to the "bottom" of the logic. In addition to the graphic layout of the structure, the diagramming technique limits the complexity of a single program unit through the way it occupies space on the page. There really is no way to have a multi-page Nassi-Shneiderman chart. Use of the Nassi-Shneiderman diagramming technique forces programmers to develop small pieces of code, and this has the wonderful effect of reducing errors.

But now the bad news. Nassi-Shneiderman charts take a long time to draw, and the only way to maintain them is to redraw them. There is no automated technique that supports the diagrams at present, although some projects have rigged up collections of boxes and decision spaces. The graphics support available on microcomputers such as the Apple Macintosh® makes the job easier, but not as simple as it should be.

Despite the disadvantages in terms of speed, the benefits of Nassi-Shneiderman diagrams are such they should be considered as a standard tool in the crunch-mode project. This is particularly true for library programs in the system. The additional accuracy in the programming process these diagrams can provide is worth the extra time it takes to draw them.

The standard reference for Nassi-Shneiderman diagrams is the paper, "Flowchart Techniques for Structured Programming," written by I. Nassi and B. Shneiderman. It can be found in the ACM Association for Computing Machinery SIGPLAN Notices of August 1973 (Volume 8, No. 8). A brief writeup can be found in *Diagramming Techniques for Analysts and Programmers* by Martin and McClure and published by Prentice-Hall. Another good description is found in *Managing the Structured Techniques* by E. Yourdon, published by Yourdon Press of New York.

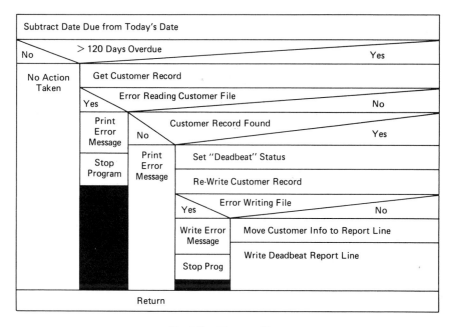

Nassi-Shneiderman Chart.

Action Diagrams

Action diagrams are an outgrowth of earlier design techniques. They have a lot to recommend them for the crunch-mode project. They use graphic elements and can be prepared and maintained quickly.

The biggest advantage of action diagrams is their range. The action diagram notation can be used from the top levels to the lowest levels of the system. The hierarchy of actions within the program is made clear by the use of brackets at different levels. The structured programming elements of sequence, selection and iteration are easy to pick out.

The brackets act as a guide through the text of the diagram. If the text is readable, the structure and details of the program can be understood without much trouble. The use of the graphic brackets seems to inhibit sloppiness in the writing of pseudocode, probably because the programmer must break away from the text on a regular basis. As a result, the programmer doesn't picture herself "writing code."

At least one automated design aid for producing action diagrams is available. It's called Action Diagrammer and it's available from DDI of Ann Arbor, Mich. It runs on IBM™ Personal Computers or compatible units. Because of the simplicity of the graphics involved, action diagrams can be produced easily on any system that supports both text and graphics. It may be possible to set them up on computers and terminals that don't support graphics per se by using combinations of normal ASCII characters like vertical bars, hyphens, and equal signs.

The recommended reference for action diagrams is *Diagramming Techniques for Analysts and Programmers* by James Martin and Carma McClure. It's published by Prentice-Hall of Englewood Cliffs, N.J. Martin and McClure also have a book devoted specifically to action diagrams. It is *Action Diagrams*, published by Prentice-Hall.

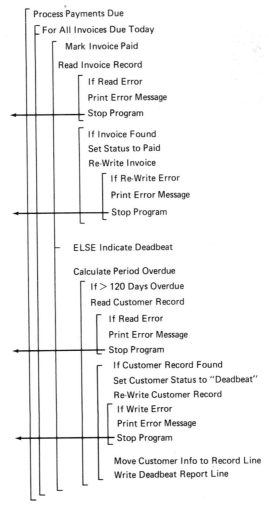

Action Diagram.

Structured English and Pseudocode

These two techniques are lumped together because of similarities in approach and their particular role in a crunch-mode environment. Each of them can be an effective *personal* design tool, but they share a weakness as *public* design tools. Neither has an explicit graphic element. This limits their effectiveness in communicating design between designer and reviewer. It's not that the ideas contained in graphic methods are better, or even that they're different—it's just faster to look at a picture and grasp the underlying design.

Structured English and pseudocode can be produced and maintained easily with standard program editors and word processors. If you are using a fourth-generation language, the keywords from the language can often be used as part of the structured English or pseudocode text. The difference between structured English and pseudocode is one of degree. In pseudocode, the iteration and decision operators often mimic the actual language used; in structured English, the operators will be more generic, and some of the lower-level topics handled explicitly by pseudocode (I/O details, for example) will be missing. While structured English uses English text exclusively, pseudocode often includes symbolic operators.

Because structured English and pseudocode "look like" the actual code and contain no graphic elements except indentation, the programmer who uses them is often seduced into thinking about code rather than design. It is common to find pseudocode and structured English designs that are incomplete, the programmer having started the actual code once she was convinced she understood the problems.

```
CHECK FOR DEADBEAT
     Subtract BILL DATE from TODAYS DATE to
          get DAYS OVERDUE
     IF DAYS OVERDUE is GE 120
          Read CUSTOMER RECORD
          Set CUSTOMER STATUS to DEADBEAT
          Write CUSTOMER RECORD
          Move CUSTOMER NAME, CUSTOMER PHONE
               and BILL AMOUNT
               to DEADBEAT REPORT LINE
          Write DEADBEAT REPORT LINE
     ELSE DO Nothing (Customer is not a
          deadbeat)
```

An Example of Structured English

There is no "official" standard for preparing structured English or pseudocode. However, books that treat structured English consistently state the importance of using the sequence, decision, and repetition structures of structured programming. Tom DeMarco in *Structured Analysis and System Specification* (Yourdon Press, N.Y.), Gane and Sarson in *Structured Systems Analysis: Tools and Techniques* (McDonnell-Douglas, Mo.), and Martin and McClure in *Diagramming Techniques for Analysts and Programmers* (Prentice-Hall, N.J.). All give discussions, rules and examples that can make your use of structured English and psuedocode more effective.

```
CHECK FOR DEADBEAT
     TODAYS DATE-BILL DATE→OVERDUE
     IF OVERDUE > 120
        READ CUSTOMER RECORD, ON ERROR→STOP
        DEADBEAT→CUSTOMER STATUS
        UPDATE CUSTOMER RECORD, ON ERROR→STOP
        CUSTOMER NAME, CUSTOMER PHONE,
            BILL AMOUNT→REPORT LINE
        PRINT REPORT LINE, ON ERROR→STOP
```

An Example of Pseudocode

Warnier-Orr Diagrams

Warnier-Orr Diagrams are very handy for representing data organization, and they can also be used for representing program logic. They are at their best when used in designing a system that is data-driven rather than processing-intensive.

Warnier-Orr diagrams lay out the data as a hierarchy of elements, and in most cases this is the easiest way to think about it. The diagrams are easy to draw and can be understood by customers without difficulty. There is no provision in the technique for representing data organizations such as third-normal form databases, but in many cases this is not a serious problem.

When Warnier-Orr diagrams are used for program logic, their unusual notation for selection and iteration may cause problems. The notation in the accompanying example is *not* the standard notation but a substitute provided to improve comprehension by those readers not familiar with the technique. Automatic code generation is possible from Warnier-Orr procedure diagrams, and this may justify spending additional time to get comfortable with the standard notation.

There is a place in every crunch-mode project for Warnier-Orr diagrams. They are an excellent tool for data design and can be produced and maintained quickly by hand. The diagrams are easily adapted to microcomputers with graphics programs that support text, and automated drawing aids are available on several computers.

The automated design aids and code generators are available through Ken Orr and Associates of Topeka, Kansas. They come with very good documentation and support, and versions are available for many different computer systems.

The standard references for Warnier-Orr diagrams are Jean-Dominique Warnier's book, *Logical Construction of Systems*, published by Van Nostrand Reinhold of New York, and Kenneth Orr's book, *Structured Systems Development*, published by Yourdon Press of New York.

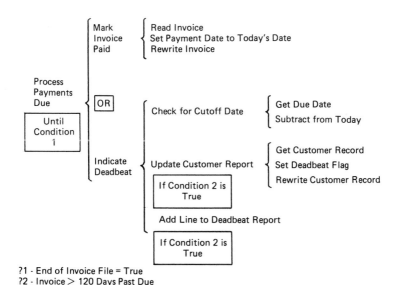

?1 - End of Invoice File = True
?2 - Invoice > 120 Days Past Due

Warnier-Orr Process Diagram.

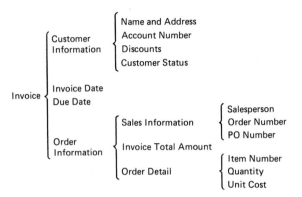

A Warnier-Orr Data Diagram.

NOTES

Chapter 1

1. F.P. Brooks, Jr., *The Mythical Man-Month*, Addison-Wesley, 1975. This remains one of the most concise and readable books on software project management. Although some of the examples may seem dated, the central themes are as current now as they were then.

2. Tom Peters and Nancy Austin, *A Passion for Excellence*, Random House, 1985. Part 3 of this book discusses innovation in depth and may give you a more positive outlook on crunch mode.

3. Alvin Toffler's book, *Future Shock* (Random House, 1970) was one of the first to recognize the effects of the rate of change in technology and society.

Chapter 2

1. John Le Carré (David Cornwell), *Smiley's People*, Alfred A. Knopf, 1980.

2. If you are new to the work of specifying systems, you should take the time to read some material on general systems thinking. Gerald Weinberg, the author of several readable books on the craft of programming, has writ-

ten three books on the topic: *An Introduction to General Systems Thinking*, John Wiley, 1975; *Rethinking Systems Analysis and Design*, Little, Brown, 1982; and, with Daniela Wienberg, *On the Design of Stable Systems*, John Wiley, 1979.

3. The concept of system essence is dealt with at length by Stephen Mc-Menamin and John Palmer in their book *Essential Systems Analysis* (Yourdon Press, 1984).Part 8 of the book, "Managing Essential Systems Analysis," gives another look at the work of "going in" when time is a constraint.

4. I was once given a project that required approval from four groups; I was also told it needed to be completed in 120 days. The specifications were rushed out the door in two weeks and passed to each of the groups for "sign off." Approval came six months later, at a point when the members of the original project team had all been reassigned to other work. Fortunately (for me, anyway), the project was given to a different project leader who presided over its eventual demise.

5. A survey of requirements methodology techniques is available in "A Fast Way to Define System Requirements" by Gary Rush. This article appeared in the "In Depth" section of *Computerworld* on October 7, 1985. Reprints may be ordered from *Computerworld* by writing to CW Communications, Inc., 375 Cochituate Rd., Box 880, Framingham, Mass. 01701.

6. Edsger W. Dijkstra, *Selected Writings on Computing: A Personal Perspective*, Springer-Verlag New York, 1982. This collection includes, among its many surprises, the observation, "The tools we use have a profound (and devious!) influence on our thinking habits, and, therefore, on our thinking abilities."

Chapter 3

1. Tom DeMarco gives an excellent introduction to the use of data flow diagrams in *Structured Analysis and System Specification*, Yourdon Press, 1978. Another good introduction is Gane and Sarson, *Structured Systems Analysis* from the IST publications group at McDonnell-Douglas.

2. Jean-Dominique Warnier and Kenneth Orr have each written books presenting the diagramming method bearing their name. Warnier's book, *Logical Construction of Systems* (translated for Van Nostrand Reinhold, 1981) and Orr's book *Structured Systems Development* (Yourdon, 1979) give excellent examples of its use. When using Warnier-Orr diagrams as part of a presentation some of the notation's details, such as the "OR" symbols, should be replaced with their natural language equivalents if they are to be used at all.

Chapter 4

1. Tom DeMarco, *Controlling Software Projects*, Yourdon Press, 1982. This is probably the best book available dealing specifically with estimating and measurement for software development. It is a readable, practical guide to developing software metrics within your organization.

2. Harold Sackman, in *Man-Computer Problem Solving* (Auerbach, Princeton, NJ, 1970), shows the results of controlled studies where the ratio of performance between the best and worst programmers was 25 to 1 for the programming task and 28 to 1 for debugging. Gerald Weinberg discusses these results and examines the basis of differences in programmer productivity in *The Psychology of Computer Programming* (Van Nostrand Reinhold, New York, 1971).

3. From F.P. Brooks, *The Mythical Man-Month*, Addison-Wesley, 1975.

4. Tom DeMarco, *Structured Analysis and System Specification*, Yourdon Press, 1978.

5. Tom DeMarco, *Controlling Software Projects*, ibid.

Chapter 5

1. This excellent example is taken from *Systems Development Without Pain* by Paul T. Ward, Yourdon Press, 1984. The book concentrates on the specification process, with particular attention to the exchange of information between the analyst and the customer.

2. George Polya, *How to Solve It*, Second Edition, Princeton University Press, 1957. Polya, a noted mathematician, provides an organized treatment of heuristics that has value even to those who are not "mathematically inclined."

3. A detailed discussion of "pathological connections" and the damage they can do can be found in E. Yourdon and L. Constantine, *Structured Design*, Prentice-Hall, 1979, in Chapter 13. "Pathological connections" are a form of "hidden interface." The called module or process is coded to use information from the caller which the caller has not explicitly passed.

4. For an introduction to PSL/PSA, see Daniel Teicherow and Ernest Hershey II, "PSL/PSA: A Computer-Aided Technique for Structured Documentation and Analysis of Information Processing Systems," IEEE Transactions on Software Engineering, Vol. SE-3, No. 1, January 1977.

5. The international telecommunication standards group, CCITT, has developed a language for specifying communications protocols using the fi-

nite state technique. The Specification·Description Language (SDL) is described in "SDL User Guidelines," Study Group XI, Working papers 3-1 and 3-4, 1977.

6. James Martin, *System Design from Provably Correct Constructs*, Prentice-Hall, 1985. This is a good introduction to the methods developed by Higher Order Software of Cambridge, Mass. It includes several excellent examples.

7. An excellent and readable book covering walkthroughs and other types of reviews is D. Freedman and G. Weinberg, *Handbook of Walkthroughs, Inspections and Technical Reviews*, Little, Brown and Co., 1982. Another book on the same subject is *Structured Walkthroughs* by E. Yourdon, Yourdon Press, 1984.

Recommended Thing to Do: If you have access to a microcomputer and a modern database package such as dBASE or RBASE, set up a little data file with four or five invoices in it and then produce a report showing the invoices, first ordered by amount due and then by date due. Once you've done that, go back and do the same thing in BASIC. Then compare your productivity.

Chapter 6

1. J. Tracy Kidder, *The Soul of a New Machine*, Little-Brown, 1981. This is an excellent book in many ways. It describes the development of the Data General Eclipse MV/8000 in a way that captures some of the flavor of this business for those not in it. The book is, however, at its best when it describes the people on the project—what they did and what the project did to them.

2. Kidder, ibid.

3. Sun Tzu, *The Art of War*, translated by Samuel B. Griffith, Oxford University Press, 1963.

4. Robert Townsend, *Up the Organization*, Alfred A. Knopf, Inc., New York, 1970.

5. Frederick P. Brooks, "The Mythical Man-Month," Addison-Wesley, 1975. Other materials on chief programmer teams can be found in Harlan Mills' book, "Software Productivity," Little Brown, 1983.

6. Kidder, ibid.

Recommended Reading—Philip Semprevivo, *Teams in Information Systems Development*, Yourdon Press, 1983. The book explores a number of workable alternatives in setting up team structures.

Chapter 7

1. N. Strung, S. Curtis, and E. Perry, *Whitewater*, Macmillan & Co., 1976.

2. In some cases, "testable" software is not enough. If the software is to be audited, it must be designed with the eventual audit in mind. If possible, the project leader should have someone from the audit group involved in the project from the first day. A software audit is an awful thing to lay on top of a crunch-mode project. I have yet to hear of one that uncovered significant new problems with a system.

3. Harlan Mills, *Software Productivity*, Little, Brown & Co., 1983. This is a collection of papers and articles written by Mills. Many of them are classics in the field of programming.

4. Terry Baker, in "Chief programmer team management of production programming" (IBM Systems Journal, Volume 11, No. 1, 1972), describes an information system that was developed for the New York Times. The system, which contained about 87,000 lines of code, was completed in a year by a three-person team. This is an early example of work by a "chief programmer team."

Recommended reading: Glenford Myers *The Art of Software Testing*, Wiley-Interscience, New York, 1979. There are many good books on writing programs and very few, good or otherwise, about testing them. Myers' book should be read by anyone seriously interested in producing high-quality software. It will be a revelation to many programmers who don't realize what a challenge it is to really test software well.

Chapter 8

1. There is a simple analogy I use in the argument against trying to maintain the original schedule. First I ask the person who is trying to keep the original schedule if he could get to a place two hundred miles away if I gave him a Corvette. Of course, he'll say yes. Then I'll ask if he can make it in an hour. He'll say no. I then point out I have given him a very fast car, fully capable of going the distance, but I have still put up some conditions that make the goal unreachable. That, I continue, is what he is trying to do with the project.

For the person who wants to add more people, I first point out that some things can't be speeded up. It takes nine months from conception to birth no matter how many women you put on the job. Second, I give him Brooks' Law: "Adding manpower to a late software project makes it later." Brooks was project manager for OS/360 and knows whereof he speaks.

INDEX

A

Account file, description of, 26
ACM, Association for
    Computing Machinery, 174
Action Diagrammer®, 175
Action Diagrams, 176
Action diagrams, 91, 92, 175–76
Ada, 90
Ad-hoc design reviews versus
    walkthroughs, 97–98
ALGOL, 88
American Totalizator Systems,
    5, 127–28
Analyst Toolkit®, 85–86, 172
APL, 87
Apple Computer, 174
Art of War, The, 108–9
Austin, Nancy, 5
Automated design aids, 31
Autotote, Inc., 5–6

B

BASIC, 87
BLISS, 90
Blueprints, use of, 69, 71
Boeing Computer Services, 19
Brooks, F. P., 114
Budget constraints, 62–63
Burnout:
    project leader, 155
    project team, 154–55
Butler Manufacturing
    Company, 82

C

C, 88
Call-a-Bet project, description
    of, 12, 15
CASE-2000®, 85, 86

Changes:
in a presentation, 36–37
in specifications, 149–51
Charts:
Nassi-Shneiderman, 91, 92, 174
structure, 173–74
CNA Insurance Co., 19
COBOL, 82, 84, 88, 90
Coding standards, 98–99
Consensus™, 19
Consultants and the project team, 115–17
Contracts:
examining, 13–14
pitfalls in, 14
specifications in, 14
Crunch-mode projects, reason for, 4
Customer:
specification changes and the, 149–51
project leader's relationship with, 17–19, 150–51
project manager's relationship with, 138

D

Data dictionaries, 74
Data flow diagrams, 15, 26, 30–31, 171–72, 173
DDI™, 175
Deadline, what to do when the project cannot meet its, 155–57
Debugging, system, 139–41
DeMarco, Tom, 44, 171, 172, 178
Design tools, descriptions of, 170
Development documentation, 161–62, 165

Product DFDdraw™, 85, 86, 172
Diagramming Techniques for Analysts and Programmers, 174, 176, 178
Diagrams:
action, 91, 92, 175–76
data flow, 15, 26, 30–31, 171–72, 173
Warnier-Orr, 16, 30, 31, 173, 178–80
Dijkstra, Edsger, 21
Documentation:
development, 161–62, 165
user, 162–63
Dynatote on-track account betting project, description of, 12, 15

E

Elegance in system development, 67, 99
Estimating:
avoiding compromise, 57–58
dive-and-surface approach to, 60, 62
failure and, 45
goal setting and, 45
percentages and, 45–46
resources and, 55–57
software, 43–45
techniques, 58–60
Excelerator™, 85, 86, 172

F

Financial incentives for the project team, 117–20
"Flowchart Techniques for Structured Programming," 174

FORTH, 90
FORTRAN, 82, 86

G

Gane, Chris, 171, 172, 178
General systems thinking, 11
GPSS, 90
Graphic abstraction, use of, 48,
     51
Graphics, importance of using,
     68

H

HOS® (Higher Order
     Software), 81, 82, 84, 90

I

IBM, 19, 172, 175
Innovation, key to, 5
Index Technology Corp.
     (InTech), 85, 86, 172, 173
Installation, systems, 165
IST®, 172

J

JAD® (Joint Application
     Design), 19

K

Kidder, Tracy, 107, 118

L

Leadership. *See* Project leader;
     Project manager
*Logical Construction of
     Systems*, 179
Lotus Development Corp., 82
Lotus 1-2-3®, 82

M

McClure, Carma, 174, 176, 178
McDonnell Douglas Automation
     Company, 85, 86, 172, 173
Machine availability as a
     resource, 56
Maintenance, systems, 165–66
*Managing the Structured
     Techniques*, 174
Martin, James, 82, 174, 176,
     178
Method®, The, 19
Milestone event(s), 58, 60
     missing a, 146–49
"Military Maxims and
     Thoughts," 113
Mills, Harlan, 133
Modules, use of, 48–49, 51, 53
MUMPS, 90
Mythical Man-Month, The, 114

N

Napoleon, 113
Nassi, I., 174
Nassi-Shneiderman charts, 91,
     92, 174
New York Times project, 133
Non-producing project team
     members, 152–54

O

Orr, Kenneth, 179
Ken Orr and Associates, 179
Outside-in approach, 93–94
Overtime for project team
    members, 117, 119, 123–
    24, 126

P

Packaging, definitions of, 71, 92
Pascal, 82, 84, 88
Passion for Excellence, A, 5
People as a resource, 55
Percentages, estimating and,
    45–46
Performance Resources, 19
Personality conflicts, 151–52
Peters, Tom, 5
PL/1, 84, 88
Post-mortem, importance of
    conducting a project, 167–
    68
Presentation:
    the project team at the, 37–38
    top-down thinking at the, 38–
    39
Problem Statement Analyzer
    (PSA), 77
Problem Statement Language
    (PSL), 77
Project leader:
    burnout of the, 155
    characteristics of the, 107–9,
        113–15, 145
    relationship with customer,
        17–19, 150–51
    responsibilities of the, 14–15,
        124, 130, 131–34, 135,
        140–41, 148–49, 166, 167,
        168

working with the project
    manager, 109–11, 151
Project librarian, responsibilities
    of the, 132–33, 135
Project manager:
    characteristics of the, 109–11,
        114–15, 137–39
    people problems and the,
        151–55
    relationship with customer,
        138
    responsibilities of the, 137–39
    working with the project
        leader, 109–11, 151
Project team:
    assembling the, 111–12
    burnout on the, 154–55
    consultants and the, 115–17
    morale of the, 135–37
    non-producing members of
        the, 152–54
    organizing the, 114–15
    personality conflicts on the,
        151–52
    post-project review of the,
        168
    the presentation and the, 37–
        38
    pressures on individual
        programmers, 103–7
    selling the project to the,
        112–14
PROLOG, 83
Prototyping tools, 92–97
Pseudocode, 91–92, 177–78
    example of, 178

R

Requirements, understanding,
    21

S

Sarson, Trish, 171, 172, 178
Schedules:
  definition of, 47
  detail and, 53
  difference between crunch-
    mode and "normal"
    project, 47–48
  graphic abstraction and, 48,
    51
  importance of, 63–64
  use of modules in, 48–49, 51,
    53
Shneiderman, B., 174
Software estimating, 43–45
Soul of a New Machine, The,
  107, 118
Specifications:
  changes in, 19
  in contracts, 14
Structure charts, 173–74
*Structured Analysis and System
  Specification,* 172, 178
Structured Design, 174
Structured English, 91–92, 177–
  78
  example of, 177
*Structured Systems Analysis:
  Tools and Techniques,* 172,
  178
*Structured Systems
  Development,* 179
Sun Tzu, 108–9
System(s):
  adding functions onto a, 15,
    17
  analysis, 6–7
  changes in, 36–37
  debugging, 139–41
  difference between
    knowledge and
    understanding of, 11–12

difference between wide and
  narrow, 33, 36
initial presentation of, 25–26,
  30
initial thinking, 11
installation, 165
maintenance, 165–66
nickname, 19
partitioning a, 33
poorly understood, 20
similarities between, 18
testing, 131–34
tools as a resource, 57
tools used in identifying
  requirements for a, 19
understanding contracts, 13–
  14
use of diagrams, 15, 16, 26,
  30–31, 91, 92, 171–72
very complex, 21
*System Design from Provably
  Correct Constructs,* 82

T

Testing:
  importance of, 126–28
  system, 131–34
  unit, 128–31
  of user training, 164
Text documentation, problem
  with, 68
Top-down thinking, importance
  of, 38–39
Totalizator, definition of, 15
Townsend, Robert, 110
Training, user:
  development of, 163–64
  difference between user
    documentation and, 163
  testing of, 164
Transaction processing
  systems, 33

U

Unit testing, 128–31
Universal Module Tester, 130
Up the Organization, 110
USE.IT®, 82
User documentation:
  difference between training
    and, 163
  importance of, 162–63
User training. *See* Training,
  user

W

Walkthroughs versus ad-hoc
  design reviews, 97–98

Warnier, Jean-Dominique, 179
Warnier-Orr:
  diagrams, 16, 30, 31, 173,
    178–80
  methods, 71
Weinberg, Gerald, 11
Whiteboard and colored
  markers, use of, 85
Wisdm®, 19
Wise, Inc., 19

Y

Yourdon, E., 174
Yourdon, Inc., 85, 172, 173
Yourdon-Constantine structured
  design, 71, 174